Wince: A Pun on Thyme

Scientifically Crafted Tales

Hope this is a source of fun and amusement.

Love, Lou

Lou Lippman

Thanks go to longtime friend Bob Boice for exhorting me, way back when, to write for *Worm Runner's Digest*, which provided my first outlet since high school for publishing humorous articles. The author expresses appreciation to his research collaborators who helped with the studies that provided the empirical base for the structure of these stories: Mara Dunn, Ivan Sucharski, Kristine Bennington, and Sarah Tragesser. They are in no way responsible for any of these tales; the blame resides entirely with me.

I thank my family for putting up with the type of person who would compose this kind of material. My granddaughter, Denali, seems to recognize when I am preoccupied (composing nonsense in my head) and my daughter, Leah, graciously pretends to appreciate her father's style of humor. My most stoic wife, Marcia, provided invaluable feedback on these stories, catching inconsistencies of all types. Special thanks go to my son, David, who actually expressed appreciation for some of the tales. He was most patient, generously dealing with all matters involved with seeing this beast into print: Advice, formatting, cover design, layout, etc.

Additional copies are available through Amazon.com or CreateSpace
ISBN: 978-1490447148

Back cover photo courtesy Millie Johnson

Foreword

Most readers will ignore this section and just skip to the stories, saving themselves the tedium and aggravation associated with academic concerns. If they do, they'll just miss a couple tales, a few Tom Swifties, and some obscure information. If they don't, they might delude themselves into thinking that they got a bit of an education.

Stories leading up to a pun or having a pun in the punch line are a quite common form of wordplay, and have been available from a huge variety of sources. Let's consider a couple examples that have been in public domain for ages.

Remember the story of the king of a tropical island who had a special chair made for him each year? With the arrival of each new chair, he stored the previous one in the attic of his palace—a typical dwelling made of hay, sod, and with palm fronds for a roof. Eventually the weight from so many royal stools in the attic was so great that a windstorm caused the entire place to come crashing down, killing the king. The moral of the story: People who live in grass houses shouldn't stow thrones.

This was a popular story and it is amusing because of the word substitutions in the punch line. It is like another story about an alien creature from outer space that had the weird appearance of being covered from head to toe with green hair and with a pointed head that resembled a hypodermic needle. People called it the furry with the syringe on top. That punch line consists of a spoonerism (sound substitution) just as does the final two words of the story about the king.

Both are cute and amusing. But I contend that they are a bit weak. The story about the king winds up with a distorted aphorism about criticizing others for the deficiency that you, yourself, possess. (The pot calling the kettle black.) But nowhere in the story is there any reference to that general idea. The proverb is simply tossed out, in isolation. Similarly for the space creature story, which ends in a familiar phrase, provoking a bit of surprise and amusement. But it, too, is in isolation—without reference to the musical play that was the source of the phrase, or even without reference to a horse-drawn vehicle. There were simply word substitutions, as seen with "knock-knock" jokes (and in the title of this book). My intuition was telling me that these types of fables would be more clever and coherent if that second thread of information could be woven into the tale. As a further example, versions of the following pun came to circulate:

> A holy man in India walked barefoot everywhere, to the point that the soles of his feet became quite thick and hard. Due to advanced age and an unwholesome diet, he became quite thin and frail with very foul breath. He was known as a super calloused fragile mystic hexed with halitosis.

Obviously, this is an exceptionally clever composition. But there is no reason for the pun on superfragilisticexpialidocious. Consider this modified version:

> Mary Poppins had an audience with a holy man in India, who walked everywhere, to the point that the soles of his feet were thick and hard. Mary was quite put off by his thin and frail appearance and very foul breath. Upon returning to London from her travels, friends asked Mary about her meeting with the venerable master. In her typically upbeat and honest fashion, she replied enthusiastically, "Super calloused fragile mystic hexed with halitosis."

My intuition told me that building this additional contextual connection to the punch line not only made the entire tale more coherent, but also made it more clever and funny. Pun humor almost invariably arises from incongruity—features that have a similarity—dissimilarity quality. But if the incongruity is also *appropriate*, then it is particularly amusing, as Elliott Oring, a major expert on humor, has suggested. In other words, if something can be both congruous and incongruous at the same time, it tends to be funny; that humor arises from discovery of connections between "underlying oppositions."

I believe that I had put that intuition to work in high school when I'd written a take-off of an Aesop-type fable, where the moral at the end of the story was a pun. I had definitely incorporated contextual connections when writing Poor Richard's Abstracts—my "contribution" to the country's bicentennial. These were bogus research abstracts that led to puns, most of which were based on the types of aphorisms that Ben Franklin had collected. I also put this "principle" to work in a story in my introduction to "Clonundrums," a collection of deliberately "terrible" gags based on cloning. For example, Q: What kind of perfume is made from budded organisms? A: Eau de Clone. Here is that story, reprinted from *The Journal of Irreproducible Results*, which can be seen as a modification of a pun that had been floating in the public domain:

> Placing some cells scraped from his tongue into a Petri dish, a geneticist grew a copy of himself. Although his duplicate was a perfect physical match, it had one ironic behavioral quirk: a foul mouth. After two years of constant embarrassment from the incessant barrage of gross verbiage, the geneticist decided to put an end to it. Under the guise of a sightseeing excursion, he lured his duplicate to the top of a skyscraper and, despite the presence of lots of other tourists, pushed his lewd nemesis over the edge to its death. Mercifully, the indecent screams on the way down were its last.
>
> The cause of the copy's demise was surely not ambiguous: the presence of witnesses was no problem either. Still, this event raised some surprising legal issues beyond the obvious question of how the murder of

> a duplicate is any different from trimming a fingernail and discarding the parings. In this case, a jurisdictional dispute arose. The homicide division of the local police contended that it should be in charge of all investigations and legal proceedings, culminating in a felony indictment. But some federal agencies asserted not only that they should have responsibility, but also that the accusation should be less severe. The upshot of all this quibbling was that the Federal Communications Commission was given full authority for prosecuting the case, charging the geneticist with a misdemeanor. At first blush, this outcome seems absurd—until realizing after all that the geneticist was, in fact, guilty of making an obscene clone fall.

Contextual connection clearly adds to the cleverness and humor of the punch line. Now let us consider another element that contributes to humor value. Jokes, gags, and riddles are all like little problems to solve. And there seems to be some optimal level of difficulty or "remoteness," so if either too difficult or too easy, the humor is dampened. Let's refer to the initial story above. Suppose that the king's dwelling had been described in the body, or set-up, of the tale as a grass house. And suppose that the word "throne" had appeared, rather than the words that had been used instead (stool, chair). My bet is that the redundancy with the punch line would have weakened its punch, and weakened the humor. Likewise for the space-alien story, if the creature had been described as furry with a head like a syringe. The reader needs to devote a little bit of effort in order to "connect the dots" and "fill in the blanks." Otherwise, humor is lost. However, huge effort to make connections simply leads to bewilderment. So there is need for a bit of problem solving leading to discovery—which can be aided with additional contextual connections. Can you see how the Indian holy man story could be weakened with less judicious word choice?

Here's yet another quick example:

> Q: What do you call a snake that rides around on the front of a car?
>
> A: A windshield viper.

Consider what happens with redundant language.

> Q: What do you call a viper that rides around on your car's windshield?

And consider what happens when connections are too obscure.

> Q: What do you call a reptile that rides on your car?

As an additional example, consider the following excellent one-liner:

> "I used to play the trombone, but I let it slide."

Note the need to supply a little information for problem solving. Note also how you can "deconstruct" this gag to nonsense by replacing "used to" with "currently"; "trombone" with "trumpet"; and "let it slide" to "let it go." I contend that there seems to be a continuum, ranging between excessive redundancy and excessive obscurity, where an ideal amount of association results in a suitable amount of problem solving and an optimal degree of perceived humor. Another of the "inverted U" relationships that keep cropping up in many circumstances involving processing of information.

These various ideas were actually put to empirical test in order to take them beyond personal intuition and toward a principle of humor. That means research. And research typically means taking something interesting and becoming analytic with it to the point of spoiling it. So it has to be expected that research on humor would be tedious and rather boring. But its outcomes could serve as guidance for production of stories that were especially clever and amusing. For the curious and not faint-hearted, let me illustrate what we did.

First, we wanted to focus and simplify. For that reason, we used one type of one-line (one-sentence) material: Tom Swifties, which can be found by the ton on the internet, some good and some not so good. Swifties came about as a lampoon of a particular sentence structure that seemed to happen with excessive frequency in the Tom Swift stories. Each sentence had the basic structure, "'Statement,' said Tom, adverb." As simple one-line gags, the humor arose due to a connection between a word in the sentence and the adverb. Note that these items definitely are not rollicking, fall-off-your-chair and roll-on-the-floor-with-laughter types of humor. They are just clever little items that provoke little more than a smile as a mirth reaction, typical of wordplay rather than jokes. But because they are so brief, it is easy to see the elements at work. Here is a typical example:

> "This is a very good place to put our camp," said Tom tentatively.

So what's clever or slightly amusing? The connection between the word "camp" and the adverb at the end of the sentence, which virtually serves as a little punch line. The incongruity comes from the disparity between meanings of the word "tentatively" and the "tent" that you would use when camping. Considering the problem-solving comments made earlier, can you see what would happen if one word were changed?

> "This is a very good place to put our tent," said Tom tentatively.

The reader no longer has to go through a thought process to connect an implement of camping and part of the adjective. As a result of this redundancy, the humor and cleverness is weakened (if not destroyed). Let's consider yet another possibility:

> "This might be a good place to put our camp," said Tom tentatively.

By adding a shade of doubt (with the word "might"), a contextual connection is established between the statement and the adjective. As a result, there is greater overall coherence and there is a contribution to the appropriateness of the incongruity. And in keeping with what we learned through some actual studies, an increase in reports of humor and cleverness. (Note that all humor could easily be destroyed by changing the adjective [e.g., to gratefully] or the key word in the sentence [e.g., coats]). Let's have a few more illustrations of Swifties that require this tiny bit of problem solving plus coherent context:

> "I suppose I like modern painting," said Tom abstractly.
> "I definitely know that I got only the first three wrong," said Tom forthrightly.
> "Oh goody, the power is off," said Tom delightedly.
> "I'll do the right thing and pay the customs charges," said Tom dutifully.
> "Thanks for putting the burgers on the barbecue," said Tom gratefully.

It should be noted that brevity is an important part of humor with one-liner gags (but not more lengthy material). So when we did our experimentation with Swifties, we made sure that versions with and without contextual connections had the same number of words. We not only ran studies testing Swifties, but we also put these same ideas to work with the types of little stories that you will find in these pages—all with confirmatory results. Providing additional context actually did not lead to anticipation of the punch line, which would have reduced perceived humor. Instead, it made the final sentence better connected to the information in the story, increasing the appropriateness of the incongruity to be resolved.

So these tales were "scientifically engineered," but their construction was also driven by intuition. Do remember that virtually no pun material results in rollicking belly laughs. Rather, a good pun is "awful," and when effective, it results in a groan. In that respect, this book is perfect for patients recovering from surgery. Each fable is short, requiring no memory from page to page. And no stitches will be torn loose from violent laughter. The good part is that you, the reader, are spared all the nuisance and development. So enjoy. I do believe that all these tales are original, at least that is the intention; but with a world full of punsters, originality cannot be guaranteed.

Selected References

Lippman, L.G. (1976). Poor Richard's Abstracts (Part 1). *The Worm Runner's Digest, 18*, 78-81.

Lippman, L.G. (1977). Poor Richard's Abstracts (Part 2). *The Worm Runner's Digest, 19*, 62-65.

Lippman, L. G. (1984). Clonundrums. *Journal of Irreproducible Results, 30*, 24-25.

Lippman, L.G., Bennington, K., & Sucharski, I.L. (2002). Contextual connections to puns in Tom Swifties. *Journal of General Psychology, 129*, 202-208.

Lippman, L.G., & Dunn, M.L. (2000). Contextual connections within puns: Effects on perceived humor and memory. *Journal of General Psychology, 127*, 185-197.

Lippman, L.G., Sucharski, I.L., & Bennington, K. (2001). Contextual connections to puns in fables: Perceived humor. *Journal of General Psychology, 128*, 157-169.

Lippman, L.G., & Tragesser, S.L. (2005). Constructing something funny: Levels of associative connection in Tom Swifties. *Journal of General Psychology, 132*, 231-242.

Oring, E. (1989). Between jokes and takes: On the nature of punch lines. *Humor, 2*, 349-364.

Oring, E. (1992). *Jokes and their relations*. Lexington, KY: The University Press of Kentucky.

Oring, E. (1995). Appropriate incongruities: Genuine and spurious. *Humor, 8*, 229-235.

Tragesser, S.L., & Lippman, L.G. (2005). Puns and near puns in fables. *Journal of General Psychology, 132*, 243-254.

The Tales

In memory of my dad, Robert, and his father, Oscar, who surely contributed to my appreciation of humor--good and bad, clean and dirty.

An avowed maverick was shopping in a thrift store for a small stuffed animal toy. What caught her eye was a selection of knitted amphibians—frogs, salamanders, etc.—in a wide variety of colors and sizes. Being a dedicated nonconformist, she chose a toy having colors that deviated grossly from whatever would ever be found in nature, and also aimed for the toy that seemed to be in newest condition. As would be expected, she chose the toad less raveled.

A newly discovered cache of Warhol paintings was to be put on exhibit for the first time. Rather than soup cans, all paintings in this collection were of soft drink cans, bottles, and cartons. The museum curator responsible for the exhibit knew that the typically austere, refined chamber music normally played during an opening reception would not be suitable background music for this exhibit. In a sudden inspiration he found an endless tape that played, “Pop Goes The Easel.”

In an effort to get some rest and relaxation, a team of medical experts and a group of intelligence staff decided to pool their resources and charter a sports fishing boat for an expedition. One of the intelligence personnel—more correctly, a secret agent—had a tiny container, made to look a mole, which he always wore attached to the same place on his cheek. This hollow mole was used to conceal and transport secret documents which had been reduced photographically to microscopic dimensions.

Just as people were settling down to some serious fishing, the spy carelessly brushed his cheek, knocking his artificial mole overboard; regrettably, this conveyance had been loaded with some crucial material. To make matters even worse, as soon as the mole hit the water it was devoured in one gulp by a dogfish that happened to be cruising in the vicinity.

The agent was panic-stricken. That information was irreplaceable. Just catching the dogfish would be a problem. But even if it could be caught, it would be essential to retrieve the mole within 20 seconds, before powerful digestive juices had a chance to take effect. Furthermore, locating a small item in the innards of a fish would be no mean feat.

Somehow one of the physicians grasped the full import of the situation as soon as the spy emitted his first squawk of anguish. The doctor grabbed a net, landed the dogfish; immediately pulled out a knife, opened up the fish, reached directly into the animal's gut and pulled out the mole and its contents—unharmed. The spy was not just grateful, but was astonished—not only at the speed at which the physician understood the problem and reacted, but also at his skill in locating and retrieving the mole. The agent was particularly curious and so asked how the doctor seemed to know precisely where to look. "Oh really," the physician replied modestly, "It was just a dot in the shark."

A nut and spice farm occupied some lovely rolling countryside. Once during a freezing rain storm, the farmer's pet rabbit wandered out and had last been seen heading toward the pickling spice plots. Everyone on the farm was frantic because many of those young plants resembled carrots. The damage from the rabbit's foraging could far exceed any wreckage from the storm.

The straw boss was adamant in his instructions to his workers: "Get out there and find Beatrice and keep looking even if it takes all night. Check everywhere; search over dill and hail."

A terrible tragedy struck at the spectacular estate of an enormously wealthy tycoon. Vandals had gotten past the security devices, had unfolded all the lawn furniture, and slashed it to ribbons. Although it amounted to a comparatively trivial financial loss, this tycoon resented being victimized, and swore vengeance, vowing that he would find the culprits and would insist upon compensation, reparation, and punishment. He was careful not to touch a thing, ensuring that all evidence would be intact and as informative as possible. Being willing to spare no expense, he contacted and retained a world-famous detective who had a reputation for solving even the most elaborate and intricate intrigues quickly. True to form, the famous detective arrived, took one look at a shredded lawn couch, sneered haughtily, and said knowingly, "This is an open and cut chaise."

There once was a famous sculptor who, for a diversion from the usual geometrics, blobs, and nudes, became involved in production of a nature series. Within this series, he ended up expending his greatest energies on an Oregonian scene depicting a stand of evergreens as backdrop for a family of foraging ground squirrels. Having worked out the poses to provide proper balancing of his scene, he spent endless hours lovingly producing a sculpture in clay; he then constructed a mold and proceeded to cast a series of numbered originals in bronze. He then devoted himself to smoothing off imperfections and making finishing touches before adding his personal mark for authentication.

But to his horror and disappointment, when he put his bronzes before the public for view and sale, he found himself overrun with tourists who proceeded to degrade his efforts by making comments about fireproof pinecones, the oversize paperweight, or by giggling childishly about gopher traps or cute chipmunks. Needless to say, he was crestfallen and heartbroken. But what else could you expect when you cast squirrels before pine?

As a result of an extended history of bear-related incidences, the Parks Department assembled a team of experts. They were assigned the task of developing a special breed of bear that would be docile and friendly toward humans, refuse to accept handouts, and also have an aversion to prowling through garbage. In recounting the frustrations arising from repeated failure, the long-suffering geneticist who was heading the project was surprisingly tranquil and philosophical. He reminded his co-workers continually that failures had to be expected; that if they were not facing this impossible problem, then it would merely be some other one that was equally infeasible. He suggested that the entire enterprise could be seen as a rather typical and representative "slice of life," in that everyone has a bear to cross.

There once was a fellow who had spent years changing jobs and roaming around. Being desperate for funds, he tried to present himself as a solid and responsible citizen to the manager of a sausage company. He was hoping that he and his horse could be hired to take a wagon to various farmers in order to collect hog jowls.

The manager, however, was very shrewd. By merely observing the horse's habitual, ambling gait, he refused to hire the man, inferring not only that the horse moved too slowly (which could risk spoilage) but also that the horse's owner was unlikely to be a stable or lasting employee. In expressing his negative hiring decision, he was simple and blunt, stating that a strolling roan gathers no maws.

Once upon a time there was a young lady who had associated herself with a traveling comedy troupe for several years. This arrangement allowed her to eke out a meager existence; enough funds to avoid starvation, to obtain substandard shelter, and to procure some ratty second-hand clothing. Eventually she became fed up with this desperately impoverished existence and took steps toward improving her lot. Surveying her personal resources she came to the conclusion that her only skills were theatrical, derived from extended contact with her comedian colleagues.

Noting that employment opportunities in conventional channels seemed limited (if not closed out), she decided to gamble on non-traditional religious practices as a means for seeking upward mobility. Capitalizing on her dramatic talents, she proceeded to found a coven of hags and sirens dedicated to the practice of black magic and sorcery. In an astoundingly short time her enchanting personal charm resulted in extremely successful proselytizing. The growing demand for membership, despite exorbitant initiation fees and dues, resulted in her sponsorship of several branch covens (tax free, of course) over which she maintained total control. The fabulous wealth resulting from her courageous venture stands as testimony of her transformation from wags to witches.

Once there was an old Victorian mansion, replete with gingerbread, porches, gables, and lots of peculiar-shaped rooms with cubbyholes. But the "golden age" for this spectacular structure was in the dim past, and over the years it came to serve as a run-down residence for two sorts of inhabitants: solicitous elderly ladies—usually grandmotherly sorts who loved children—and a variety of thieves and swindlers. Surprisingly these disparate groups managed to thrive in harmony under one roof.

All was placid until a robbery took place during which some valuable jewelry had been taken. Circumstantial evidence led the authorities to suspect that one of the inhabitants was the culprit, and that the stolen goods were hidden somewhere on the premises. Therefore a warrant was issued to the police allowing a search to be conducted of all residents and the premises. The officers could see that they had a huge task given the complexity and size of the mansion in addition to the number of people involved. But their captain exhorted them to remain alert, proceed slowly and try not to miss anything, but to be careful and systematic, and to search every crook and nanny.

An enterprising little company discovered a way to manufacture surfboards in a novel way, using some disgustingly yucky industrial waste products. These boards were not only inexpensive, but they were also lightweight, strong, and exceptionally maneuverable. The only obvious problem was appearance: there was no way to eradicate or conceal the color of the material from which they were constructed. Despite the advantages of these boards, the cliquish community of surfing purists refused to be impressed, and haughtily declined to put them to a test. They declared that surfboards could only be made one way, and that others were merely cheap and disposable toys for children. These disparaging comments from the "prestigious experts" certainly did not help the company's sales. To add to the company's marketing woes, a few boards were discovered to have an internal bubble which had formed during casting. Boards having this flaw were safety hazards because they could shatter during stress.

Although matters seemed hopeless, a company designer discovered that defective boards readily could be identified by tapping and listening for a distinctive, telltale hollow resonance. As a result of this discovery, the company mounted a new advertising campaign in the form of a product warning as well as a rejoinder and challenge to the recalcitrant purists: "Don't try it if you haven't knocked it."

In his youth and long before his considerable fame, Roy Rogers used to chase outlaws by riding atop a gigantic rabbit. Although it was perfectly effective transportation, Roy was embarrassed by this deviation from the cowboy-hero norm. He was very sensitive and would fly into a rage at the slightest sign of ridicule. You might say that, at the time, he had a hare Trigger.

Initiated in New York, a particular publication began as an informal newsletter, but subsequently evolved into a complete, specialized scientific periodical. Due to its subject matter, there was editorial insistence upon the use of elevated and technical expression to avoid any accusation of crudity or sensationalism. This journal was devoted to the classification and documentation of various paroxysmal attacks, spells and convulsions which had never been described previously in published form. Naturally, this periodical had as its motto: "All the Fits That's New To Print."

A flamboyant gambler who had played high-stakes poker for years finally realized that he had a gambling addiction. He joined a support group in order to get help in stopping this risky and stressful activity. As a substitute undertaking he devoted himself to gardening. He took the energy that he previously had squandered on gambling and spent it on learning about different plants and their requirements for sunlight, particular soil composition, moisture, etc. Because he became so knowledgeable, he easily qualified for being designated officially as a master gardener, giving advice to people who consulted him for help. But he was never able to break completely with his former ways. For example, when a farmer asked a really trivial question about his wheat fields, the ex-gambler flopped a brochure on the desk and said defiantly, "Weed 'em and reap!"

There was a festival in India during which the mahouts honored their animals. They would spend several days grooming their elephants, decorating them and dressing them up with the goal of having the most splendid and elegant animal of all. Not only were the elephants decked out in costly and elaborate harnesses and headdresses, their toenails trimmed and polished, and trunks cleaned and shined, but a great part of the process involved painting the entire elephant with flowers, paisley patterns, or even some religious or landscape scenes.

One of the mahouts, named Rama McTavish, equipped his animal with kilts and a head-to-toe plaid paint job that duplicated the tartan of his clan. The other mahouts were shocked at how gross and garish his animal looked, and referred to his elephant as one genuine tacky derm.

An intellectual arranged speaking tours in which he urged people to maximize their cognitive capabilities. He advocated learning new skills, reading, and keeping mentally sharp by working puzzles of all sorts. He held workshops for the elderly, admonishing them to use these tactics to maintain their intellectual aptitude. Unfortunately, this crusader had a frustrating weight problem. Although he was highly self-disciplined in many areas of his life, it nevertheless seemed that no matter what diet he tried or the level of exercise that he imposed on himself, he simply kept increasing in girth. It certainly came as no surprise when he lamented, “A waist is a terrible thing to mind.”

An escort service in Italy advertised that they would do anything to accommodate a customer's whims. Their personnel would don any costume and they would decorate their vehicles in any fashion in order to accommodate the taste of any customer who hired their services. The real function of their service was to escort vehicles bearing important visitors to the Vatican so the luminaries could have an audience with the pope. In actuality all they did was ride in front of the passenger's taxi and honk their horns in a feeble effort to clear away other traffic on the road. This practice was consistent with their motto in their advertisements: "We toots you to a See."

Once there was an old prospector who was unshakable in his quest for semiprecious gems. Because most of his career had been that of abject failure, he had always been an eccentric and the victim of much name-calling. After decades of futile searching, something snapped—and he started laying claims to gravel pits where nothing of value was left. To make matters worse, he began to develop a variety of paranoid beliefs. For one, he began to suspect that thieves were trying to steal his heaps of broken rock. But these were not just ordinary claim jumpers. In his demented fantasies, these were, on the one hand, grafted descendants of old enemies and, on the other, members of exclusive social groups that had rebuffed him and treated him with snobbish disdain. He also imagined that these intruders were in control of flocks of trained parrots that not only continued the verbal abuse but had been taught to fly at him in squadrons to harass him and chase him from his claims.

But the old fellow was resolute and spent his days in the hills protecting his property. Occasionally, when the hallucinations began anew and were especially compelling, he could be seen shaking his fist and heard shouting the old childhood retort: "Cliques and clones may stake my stones, but birds will never herd me!"

Once there was a fellow who specialized in breeding the pariahs of the animal world—all manner of creepy bugs, vermin, etc. It was like a flea circus, but was actually a weird zoo. All was progressing satisfactorily until he noticed that his louse colony was declining in population. This was cause for serious concern since his zoo would be inadequate without a flourishing louse exhibit. As a result, he became depressed and saw himself as a failure—to the point of doubting whether his very existence was in any way worthwhile.

The breeder frantically tried to identify the cause of the problem in his louse colony. He modified their diet to no avail; likewise humidity, temperature, light duration and cycle, etc. Nothing seemed to work. But then he noticed that the healthiest of the remaining specimens were located under the only part of the available vegetation which was fresh; those living under dried or decaying fronds were weak and scrawny. The owner was thankful and pleased to get a new leaf on lice.

A gentleman who worked in a carnival as a freak (biting the heads off live chickens), exposed the techniques of several confidence schemes to police detectives for no apparent reason. It was suspected that he was ingratiating himself with the local law enforcement authorities in order to secure immunity from prosecution for his present mode of employment as well as other, more heinous, crimes he had committed in the past. As a result, the police reminded themselves of the old adage: Beware of geeks baring grifts.

A high-minded Boston matron was shocked and embarrassed to learn that despite the best of upbringings and solid moral training, her daughter had dropped out of school and was sharing housekeeping in another Massachusetts city; that is, she was living with a "common laborer" without benefit of the formal process of matrimony. The dowager mother was also upset at her daughter's means of self support. Despite the best education and training in the arts, the girl preferred to eke out a living as a beachcomber, screening the sand along Massachusetts Bay in search of coins or any lost article that could be converted into cash.

The mother tried to keep her emotions in check when socializing with her friends. But her daughter’s primary social and moral faux pas dominated her thoughts. Despite her resolute efforts at self control, on one occasion, in response to a superficial, obligatory inquiry, "How's your daughter doing," she lost control and blurted out, "Oh, she's sieving in Lynn."

A congressman, concerned about overcrowding in prisons, was reading a report about an antiquated aircraft carrier that was going to be scuttled. An idea popped into his head. It occurred to him that the carrier could easily be converted into a floating jail and, once on the high seas, society would be as safe as if the inmates were isolated on Alcatraz. He speculated about setting up farming on board in addition to other self-sustaining jobs such as fishing, to minimize expenses to the government.

He excitedly drew up a proposal specifying the structural modifications that should be made and urging that all convicts and prostitutes should be transferred on board at the earliest opportunity. Naturally the proposal had to go to committees where one quite cogent concern was raised: it would be crucial to determine whether the proposed cargo and ship modifications would exceed the vessel's capacities, pressing it dangerously below the waterline. Speaking as a typical bureaucrat, the committee chairman intoned, "Naturally before fully implementing this plan, we'll surely have to weigh its pros and cons."

A Sanskrit scholar began to wonder whether one section of one of the four collections of sacred Hindu psalms may have been apocryphal. His suspicions about authenticity arose because there was a recurrent philosophical theme that seemed to deviate from those typically represented by the Upanishads. It seemed to resemble Western thought, as it had arisen from roots in the Middle East.

Through considerable efforts in tracing history and identifying individuals who could have distorted the hymns and prayers over the centuries, the scholar identified an individual of Semitic background who not only showed up early in antiquity but also, to the scholar's great surprise, appeared to reincarnate repeatedly over the years, advocating the same philosophy again and again. The scholar thus had his first direct experience of Veda Jew.

A professional basketball player who had set a number of scoring records retired and became a dairy farmer. He greatly enjoyed his rural and self-sustaining style of life, raising his own vegetables and milking his cows. His choice of foods, however, gave him chronic gas, which became particularly and eminently evident when he engaged in the prolonged physical exertion of making butter by hand. A sports announcer, visiting the player in order to do a short report on this retired player, summarized the situation in traditional fashion: "He churns; he toots."

A common disclaimer seen on various offers, coupons, contests, and promotions is a statement that the material may be disallowed in certain states, cities, or counties. One gentleman got himself into serious difficulties by taking that disclaimer literally, treating it as an all-purpose admonition applying well beyond just advertising ploys. Because of this misunderstanding, he snuck into a secure "no admission" area of a power plant in order to take a leak, and inadvertently peed on a high voltage line, which led to his untimely demise. He had interpreted the disclaimer in reference to his bladder: Void where prohibited.

Gretchen, one of the more important personnel at a television station, had responsibility for program scheduling. It was an extremely sensitive job because the offerings during time slots for competing stations had to be considered in addition to audience demographics. A further restriction involved the schedules of the people who came out with live, rather than taped, broadcasts. She was dealing with a decision about the sequence of two live shows to be fitted into adjacent time slots. On one show unbelievable crackpots were brought in. They were typically exposed to a nasty surprise and then egged on by a screaming audience to yell and fight—a true exercise in humiliation. The other program was one of those therapist-type programs, this one having a heavy psychoanalytic and nearly mystical orientation. Gretchen puzzled over the question of sequence until her love of Rogers and Hammerstein's music in "South Pacific" gave her the solution. She happily sang out, "Springer, then Jung Time."

A person who wrote movie reviews for a newspaper chain had a reputation for being vicious and demeaning. A film had to be an exceptional work of art in order to not be nitpicked or condemned by this individual. He was at a theater watching a new film when his temper started to rise as he became more and more angry and disgusted at what he saw on the screen. His agitation reached a point where his blood pressure shot up, producing a coronary incident. He was rushed by ambulance to a hospital where, to no one's surprise, he was listed in critical condition.

A group of men working at a famous porcelain factory in Germany used their lunch break to brainstorm how to lure local girls into their beds. These were not just simple or superficial ideas. Rather, they were elaborate and detailed strategies involving various series of activities connected to a timeline. Virtually all permutations of events were tried and tested, e.g., flowers, candy, movie, gourmet dinner, vintage wine, tickets to opera, etc. Despite all the schemes and systematic blueprints for seduction, not a single tactic proved successful, thus confirming that the best planned lays of Meissen men often go awry.

Streetwalkers were given an elaborate medical questionnaire that covered all ailments, ranging from bedsores to zygotes, in an attempt to specify whatever pattern of physical malady was associated with this specific profession. The only unanimous complain was of sore, burning feet and fallen arches.

In an effort toward remediation, the women were outfitted with prosthetic devices which were designed to protect and support their feet. These items were actually configured so they looked just like feet. They were made to resemble feet so well that observers never detected that they were being worn. Although use of these "pseudopods" required some practice, the younger hookers adapted quite readily and were able to "put their best foot forward" after just one practice session. They reported reduced fatigue and business revenue above normal. The only occasional complaint was that the heels were not sufficiently rounded. Unfortunately the older women never learned to use the devices even after several weeks of instruction, showing that you can't teach an old trick new dogs.

An isolated hamlet had been under continuous rule of a monarchy for as long as it had a written history. However, the populace was exhibiting instances of brooding anxiety and occasional outbursts of mass panic that were instigated by a rumor that the queen was unable to conceive. The implication of such a problem would be that there would be no heir to whom leadership could be passed—and there were no legal or political provisions by which a ruler could be elected or appointed. One tearful washerwoman summed up their predicament by philosophizing that "into each reign, some life must fall."

An international health organization conducted a study of childbirth conditions. It was expected that more developed countries, in which births took place in relatively sanitary conditions and under the supervision of midwives or a team of medically trained personnel, would have survival rates superior to the less advanced countries, where the women gave birth in deplorable contaminated circumstances and with no outside supervision or assistance. It was surprising to learn that the survival rates and continued health of children born under these unfavorable conditions were no different than those observed in the wealthy and technologically advanced countries. It could only be surmised that God helps those who whelp themselves.

The many customers of certain racetrack tipsters were infuriated at the poor financial consequences that they incurred when acting upon the predictions that they had purchased. As a result, they acted as a mob in an effort to exact retribution. They abducted the tipsters, stripped them, paired them up, and at gunpoint required them to deliver a beating to one another. The instruments used to administer the flogging were electrical cables (one "hot" and the other ground) with the insulation removed at the locus of impact. Thus the tipsters were not only whipped, but were painfully scorched whenever blows fell concurrently. Despite the gross brutality and clear responsibility for the obvious assault and battery, a trial resulted in acquittal for all the defendants. Their defense lawyer was able to argue to the jury's satisfaction that burn-a-tout is pair flay.

Two sibling chickens lived in the same coop on a large ranch. The female was a docile soul while the male was a totally irresponsible rake. He spent most of his time sowing what seemed to be an inexhaustible supply of wild oats. The result was that gobs of hens were laying fertile eggs. The delighted rancher, eager for an even larger number of chickens, imposed the responsibility of sitting on and hatching those eggs upon the beleaguered sister. This arrangement satisfied both the farmer and rooster, and continued for quite some time. But at last the sister's good nature wore thin and she refused to care for the misbegotten products of her sibling's sexual excesses. As she put it, "Am I my keeper's brooder?"

The father of psychoanalysis had a brother living in the Southeast United States. This brother also had given considerable thought to psychosexual development, but was afraid of repercussions if he were to express his theories and concepts publicly. He preferred to put his energies into his small restaurant, making extremely popular local poultry dishes. His business expanded to additional outlets in other cities, providing a steady and comfortable income.

The restaurateur continued to have insights about the underpinnings of human behavior. To avoid notoriety, he passed his psychoanalytic notions along to his less cowardly brother Sigmund, who weathered the public outcry and achieved fame using concepts donated by this silent partner. When asked why his brother disavowed any interest in libido theory, Sigmund answered succinctly, but in an uncharacteristic New Jersey accent: "Kentucky Freud chicken."

A most unlikely trio ended up getting together on a fishing expedition. One fellow was a true hillbilly who spent his days in constant astonishment at every trivial matter that differed from what he had encountered in his limited experience. The next gentleman was an outright crazy. And the third was a philosopher. These three rented a large luxury craft and headed for the open ocean for some big-game sport fishing. But as soon as they started preparations for fishing, an endless series of disputes arose as to hook size, weight, how deep to fish, etc. Most remarkable was their discussion of bait. The hillbilly insisted on using rinds from salt pork since his daddy had taught him to use that in the swamps. The crazy was insisting on using popcorn because fish always gobble lots of it when they are sitting around in the evening playing gin rummy (an observation which the others questioned—in silence). The philosopher, after lengthy and ponderous soul-searching, chose to use pieces of pizza, mumbling about the greatest good and greatest numbers.

Apparently all three were correct in their selection of attractive bait, for a huge sea monster came streaming out of the depths and consumed all baits and fishing tackle; then tipped the fishermen out of their boat and swallowed them too. It is sad that the three gentlemen had so little time to appreciate how this fabulous piscatory prize had taken their bait—hick, loon, and thinker.

Long ago in the prehistoric era, a band of German savages were invading a region that we now recognize as Hungary. It was in the dead of winter, and the Hungarians were losing badly. Not only were they in short supply of troops, but their tools of war were depleted. As a result, every available person was drafted into action, including housewives, lawyers, doctors, religious leaders, etc. Determined to try fending off the invading hordes at any price and with any means, the Hungarians finally resorted to trapping rodents and freezing them in snow banks. Then, using the frozen vermin as projectiles, batted them soundly by war club, thus propelling them at the enemy.

As might be expected, this form of attack was not terribly impressive or effective. Many swings were usually required just in order to hit an invader—and usually the impact was of insufficient force to inflict any serious damage. But perhaps due to beginner's luck, a newly-drafted physician set his rodent on a small, low platform; then took a mighty swing and got off a really solid shot which landed and penetrated with deadly velocity. Ecstatic, he shouted in his heavy accent, "I just got a vole in Hun!"

A sports agent had spent two years combing and scouting through the Pyrenees in search of youngsters who showed unusual talent in the game of jai alai, the national sport. The plan was to choose the best and most promising youngsters in the entire country, and then take them to Latin America for intensive training before putting them on professional tour. There was no question that the agent, barring unforeseen circumstances, stood to earn a fortune in commissions because he had done his screening carefully and had pre-empted all competition. He housed the boys in a luxury hotel while he continued scouting and making selections. He finally had his twelve best prospects so it was time to go to the airport. As they prepared to leave the hotel for their Latin American flight, all the players were standing in one of the doorways when a truck driver suddenly lost control of his vehicle. The truck careened toward the hotel, right into the one doorway where the future jai alai stars were standing around, oblivious to any danger.

The agent was emotionally devastated due not just to the loss of life, loss to the sport of jai alai, loss of two years of patient searching and selection, but he began to blame himself. He cried out with the wisdom of hindsight that the youngsters should have been distributed among many of the doorways instead of being grouped at only one. He concluded that his experience goes to prove that you shouldn't put all your Basques in one exit.

An experienced forester had the job of training an eager youngster in the art of tree farming. The novice was indiscriminately in favor of trying to rescue every possible tree and branch. The more experienced person had a more realistic perspective, and tried to point out instances where efforts were, and were not, practical. One time they came across the trunk of a very mature tree which was obviously sick since sap was oozing out of the trunk in several places. Since it was a large tree having possible commercial value, the crusading youth was particularly drawn to waging an all-out effort at remediation. But the forester recognized the disease symptoms and tried to point out several things: that you can get trapped emotionally into continuing treatment far longer than good sense would justify; that the tree was doomed since the disease is incurable; and that the disease readily spreads to other trees, potentially jeopardizing the health of the entire forest. "As a rule," concluded the forester, "I've always found it best to let seeping logs die."

A fancy store had several specialized departments devoted to utensils for gourmet food preparation. These were further subdivided by nationality. The total store management was extremely efficiency oriented, and was particularly impressed by the salespeople in the Chinese food section. These personnel had virtually flawless records when it came to matters such as sales, marketing predictability, absenteeism, accuracy of information provided, speed to wait on customers, etc. Their efficiency and morale were unparalleled. At the store's annual meeting, the chairman of the board drew attention to these facts, and stated, "It is our goal to have the members of all departments learn their jobs so this entire store hums like a finely-tuned, well-oiled machine. I'd like to see it run like wok clerks."

The Forest Service was having serious trouble in Western Canada with insect pests. The agency tried the usual extermination procedures, but to no avail. They tried liberal applications of poisons, only to learn that the pests, through mutation, had become immune. However, one insightful geneticist suspected that these animals could have sensitivities to particular visual patterns. With a little lab experimentation he was able to show that these pests were hopelessly attracted to a specific curlicue. So he commissioned a painter to make hundreds of copies, recruited children to volunteer to carry placards, and organized a march which induced all the bugs out of their hiding places, just like the famed Piper of Hamlin had done, acoustically, with rats. However, rather than destroying the pests, the people marched their charges across the continent to Quebec; then nailed up the placards to keep the pests in town.

Strangely, the Quebecers did not object. Rather, they not only seemed to enjoy coexistence with the bugs, but also adopted the curlicue as their emblem of identity. As one resident put it, "It's our symbol of regional pride. It's our lure de fleas."

A social services agency conducted a "follow-up" survey in order to learn what happens to professional athletes once they retired from active competition. While still young (when most terminated their sports careers) the more popular individuals worked as managers or public relations officers for their ex-teams. Other famous players were hired by banking establishments or athletic equipment manufacturers as "consultants." Less notorious persons pursued professions in line with their education, e.g., law, teaching, hotel management, or automobile repair.

In addition, the survey showed that following retirement from these second vocations, most moved into a third "occupation" as general hired helpers. Almost none of this particular group of retirees showed the slightest tendency toward specialization, but rather most worked in a variety of occupations that included gardening, masonry, plumbing, carpentry, and electrical repair. The overall proportion of retirees performing odd jobs was highest for those who had the longest athletic careers.

On reading the report, most people were surprised by this last statistic. One elderly gentleman who read the report, however failed to exhibit surprise at the overwhelmingly high frequency of this second post-athletic-retirement career, performing odd jobs. This wise old man treated the results as unremarkable and completely anticipated, stating, "Of course. Handyman: that's a trade of old jocks."

A horse lover and racing enthusiast was disheartened when colts raised in his stable were uniformly unsuccessful in races because they were sickly and weak. He simply lacked adequate space to properly exercise his animals. Despite having an impeccably honest nature (he was a leader in his church and community), this stable owner began to sneak his horses to a nearby meadow so they could get adequate exercise. He knew that he was trespassing and that he had never been given permission to even walk in that field, let alone allow horses to trample it. Soon his guilt due to his dishonesty began to leave its mark; he lived with continual fear that he would be found out. Torn by guilt, he acquired a painful ulcer and developed a sizable repertoire of tics, twitches, and other symptoms.

Eventually he could stand the conflict no further, and contacted the owner of the meadow. He described his transgressions and apologized; admitted his guilt, and begged forgiveness. Luckily, the landowner was also an animal lover and granted the privilege of use of his land expressly as an exercise area for the young horses until they reached maturity. Almost immediately the fellow's symptoms subsided; his stomach felt better, his fears and guilt disappeared, and his twitches stopped. "Yes," he sighed with relief and contentment, "Concession is good for the foal."

Lorraine Sweet was a Peace Corps supervisor who had been assigned to work in India through the monsoon season. Once her tour of duty was over, she would be returning to her duties as middle-management bureaucrat in Washington. Meanwhile she had recruited Bertram Waddington-Smith, a local resident who was an offspring of a British colonial field officer, to serve as her assistant. Not only did Lorraine make excessive demands on Bertram's waking hours, but also she finagled him into the role of personal escort.

In the course of squiring Lorraine through a reception at the ambassador's mansion, Bertram met Cleopatra Lee and was utterly charmed and captivated. But being in a delicate and highly constrained position, he held his infatuation for Cleopatra in check and continued to serve Lorraine with as much enthusiasm as he could muster. When the monsoon season and the skies cleared, he dutifully delivered Lorraine to the airport and feigned an emotional farewell. Moments after her takeoff, his mood shifted completely. On his way out of the airport he was singing his favorite Johnny Nash tune: "I can see Cleo Lee now Lorraine is gone..."

A dishonest yachtsman decided to revive the days of the sea dog, raise his Jolly Roger, and commit flagrant robbery on the high seas. He was a tremendously captivating and charismatic person, and in no time had recruited a large crew of vandals and marauders. Although this modern day Blackbeard was not terribly concerned that his crew have such trademarks as hooks for hands, wooden legs, tattoos, eye patches, or parrots on their shoulders, he did want to preserve one traditional feature to symbolize the sea wolves of the glorious days of tall ships and courageous sailors. Specifically, he wanted to see each of his crew wearing at least one gold earring.

The captain did some comparison shopping at various facilities that offered to do piercing, and amazingly found a woman at a small shop that offered a huge discount: one dollar per piercing, as long as all members of the crew participated. When asked why she was willing to undercut the going price so greatly, she admitted having a soft spot in her heart for pirates and said, "I'll do almost anything for a buck an ear."

The coastal area of the Pacific Northwest is fortunate to have no poisonous reptiles. However, it boasts an indigenous species of snake that is unusual in its powerful affinity for cars. Soon after birth each of them heads for the hood where it periodically sends its body into a rather hypnotic, rhythmic motion back and forth in search of sustenance. The vigor of this activity seems associated with barometric conditions and humidity. They seem territorial, so only a limited number dwell on each vehicle; but being plentiful, can be found on virtually all automobiles in the region. Reptile specialists would probably classify the creature as a variant of a glass snake. But the locals simply refer to it as a windshield viper.

Starting in 1934, the Nissan Corporation maintained a warehouse for storing gears for its engines and transmissions. In the midst of a thunderstorm during which there was a record-setting torrential downpour, the building was struck by lightning. That strike triggered a massive explosion sending all the parts sky high. That was the day, as it became remembered, when it really rained Datsun cogs.

An elderly woman, on the brink of abject destitution, had continued to pretend that she was in control of great wealth. By playing the role of rich dowager, she was able to tease her various relatives into kowtowing to her every whim in the belief that they would be remembered in her will and be duly rewarded. Her talent at aristocratic affectations had all her children, nieces, nephews, and cousins sucking up to her and keeping her on her imaginary throne. Imagine their shock when, at the reading of her will and listing of assets following her demise, they discovered that all this time she had been putting on heirs.

A forest service employee claimed to be suffering great agony from uric acid crystals in his joints. As a result, the individual petitioned to be excused from the lengthy and arduous hikes required to improve pathways and cut fire trails. Seeking validation for his claims, his supervisor ordered blood tests. The lab results were ambiguous. The supervisor nevertheless chose to excuse the employee from jobs requiring appreciable amounts of hiking, thus giving the employee the benefit of the gout.

A secondary supporting actor seemed as though he couldn't steal enough audience recognition. As a result, he antagonized all other actors in the troupe by his incessant vamping, mugging, and upstaging during their performance parts. The other players asserted that he was robbing the applause that they deserved. They explained the need for him to limit his visibility during segments of performances where others were featured. He would promise and swear to behave properly, but despite his "sincere" vows, he would grab attention inappropriately in the very next performance. Finally the players voted to drop him from the company, declaring that they could no longer trust a claptomaniac.

A nobleman was the only person in his region who made his living by raising ducks and geese. The feathers were used for making pillows, comforters, warm jackets and sleeping bags. The nobleman was unusually tall, so that living in his ancestral quarters, a stone castle built by people about half his size, presented its difficulties. He would sometimes forget to duck when going through a door or entering a passageway. Because he typically moved quickly, he would knock himself unconscious at least once a week. On such occasions, if other servants or customers sought the nobleman, his butler would declare that his liege was count for the down.

A team of researchers was dedicated to discerning the relative contribution of genetics and environment to physiology and behavior. They initially focused on identical siblings who had been separated at birth, and tested for their physical and psychological differences in adulthood. They stayed with their original research goal but changed strategy—and cloned buttocks so they could study rears twinned apart.

Mr. Spooner had worked for years selling vintage Porsches and Volkswagens, and then branched out to include Korean cars in his dealership. He agonized over how best to market these Korean additions to his inventory. Late one afternoon he had an epiphany: He could equip the sporty Korean model with a GPS and market it as a Garmin-Kia.

Adolescence is always a difficulty passage, but a teenager in a small town was having an especially miserable time. No matter what he did, people perceived his decisions and actions as those of an imbecile. He tried to take solace in television and wound up hooked on game shows, soap operas, and re-runs. When the residents learned of his addiction, his reputation was even further damaged. It reached its nadir when the townspeople started referring to him as their ill-aged vidiot.

The Center for the Advancement of Clear and Articulate Speech and The Society for Eradication of Needless Jargon realized that they had some common goals. So under the leadership of Jason, the two organizations joined forces in their crusade to prevent the proliferation of odd terminology. Ironically, people disregarded the actual name of the newly combined organization, and simply referred to it as Jason and the argot-nots. Jason suggested that the combined entity needed not only some corporate identity, like a logo, but also a slogan or motto. To reflect the drive and vigor of their enterprise, they settled on "Never Say Cant."

The early days of the FBI seemed to consist of spectacular open warfare between the agency and notorious criminals. These confrontations often seemed to have a "wild west" quality to them such that it was not just a federal agency doing battle against so-called organized crime, but more individualized—zealous agent vs. famous crook. In these early years, during which the FBI developed the reputation that stayed with it for decades thereafter, an elderly gentleman was having a conversation with a Frenchman about the exploits of one its more notorious agents. During the conversation, the Frenchman was heard to remark, "Well, Monsieur. If you say that the famous crime-buster is your son, then you must be his father, n'cest pa?"

A music lover who was extremely sensitive to sounds was on a crusade to discourage all forms of excessive noise. Although she detested rock music, a dear friend talked her into attending a rock concert with him. She paid an exorbitant price in order sit in the center of the front row to experience a performance by an aging but still famous British rock group. Gritting her teeth, she managed to tolerate the first half hour of the intense racket by focusing on the arrogant antics of the players. But finally, she could no longer withstand the acoustic assault. She leaped to her feet, caught the attention of the musicians, and with all the flamboyance she could muster, flipped them the finger. Two of them keeled over dead within seconds. An autopsy revealed that both of these aging performers had died from an embolism provoked by intense anger in response to her insulting gesture. Considering that her actions led to the demise of the group and eliminated a source of excessive noise, it must be concluded that she killed two stones with one bird.

A group of college frat boys were conducting their obligatory razzing of more serious and dedicated students. Their major target was the prototypical computer geeks. They talked incessantly among themselves about the great variety of malicious pranks they would like to pull. One stuffy classics professor overheard their plotting, which he looked upon as nothing beyond fantasizing, and commented, "facta, non verba, as if any of you 'students' would know what that phrase means."

Motivated to show the professor that they were not complete ignoramuses, they decided to follow the advice. The frat boys sought out the wimpy grinds and took steps to identify each of them visually: They glued tiny round patches of wild plant life onto the foreheads of all of the computer geeks on campus. Then sought out the classics professor to report: "Weeds dot nerds!"

There once was a troupe of performing gnomes who had spent great effort trying to create a coherent show. Their intention was not just to entertain, but to attempt to deliver a social message through a skit. These trolls had a number of social goals, such as greater acceptance for all sorts of mythical beings, sprites, elves, etc., as well as for environmental sensitivity, recycling, and so on. The quality of their performance hinged on getting a recalcitrant young demon who had dismal theatrical skills to play his part convincingly. After displaying their talents to an agent, they asked hopefully, “Do you think we’ll ever make an impact?”

Politicians from opposing parties seemed to have backed themselves into competing and incompatible stances on every single issue that arose, no matter how trivial. Not only were major issues tabled and threats of filibuster flying, but there were heated debates over sizes of paperclips and the brand of hand soap in washrooms.

Because debates were continuing far into the evening, it was suggested that some of the delegates should be sent out to buy ingredients so pizzas could be concocted by the kitchen staff. Once again, the warfare about what the toppings should be fell along party lines, with one side arguing passionately for anchovies and the other railing against; one side for mushrooms, the other against; likewise for pepperoni, onions, green pepper. A few compromises finally were negotiated. Then came the choice about type of cheese: mozzarella, gorgonzola, romano? Astonishingly, there was immediate unanimity. The decision was buy parmesan.

Cases and cases of books by the famous English novelist, Arthur St. John, were loaded into the cargo hold of a freighter. These cases not only started shifting, but actually began to float in the bilge due to a leak that had failed to be detected before leaving port. Should the ship encounter a storm or rough seas, their unpredictable movement could create a hazardous situation for the ship.

On learning about these unstable boxes of literature, the captain ordered some seamen into the hold. In a brusque, no-nonsense, military fashion he barked out orders to collect heavy objects, such as spare donkey engines and anchor chain. Then the captain proceeded to issue additional gruff commands, stating precisely how to set that material on top of the floating tomes in order to stabilize them. One of the seamen, sweating profusely from the heavy labor, declared, "He really knows how to weigh down the Waugh."

Despite what would appear to be great vulnerability due to the absence of any protective shell, a species of mollusk has shown exceptional endurance and evolutionary success. Because it has a reputation as a tremendously destructive garden pest, considerable folklore had developed on how to trap and kill it and several companies were manufacturing and selling poison bait. None of those measures were the slightest bit effective, however, and the mollusks continued to thrive and wreak damage.

A small beetle made his living by delivering inspirational and motivational lectures. He was lecturing about the mollusks' exceptional survival success to a colony of uncharacteristically lazy pismires. He was ranting and raving, berating the insects on their sloth. Winding his diatribe to a fevered pitch, the beetle intoned his major message, "Look to the slug, thou ant herd."

In the days of the Wild West, an owl wound up living on a sailing vessel that worked off the California coast. This owl found plenty of vermin right on board, so never left the ship and was appreciated for keeping the rat population under control. The sailors considered him the ship's mascot and named him Wyatt after the famous lawman. This owl was most unusual in having the ability to communicate with the sailors. Unfortunately, most of Wyatt's stentorian outbursts were negative and annoying. The irritation came not just from the loudness of his speech, but also from content. Wyatt was the most thoroughly honest and blunt creature the sailors had ever encountered. He loudly broadcasted the unalloyed facts, with no regard for tact. The sailors all agreed that when it comes to the unvarnished truth, Wyatt always hoots from the ship.

The beliefs and practices of a highly devout rancher had unexpectedly rubbed off onto a family of donkeys that he owned. One day the religious rancher discovered that his donkeys had disappeared. Evidently the mother, father, and offspring had all wandered off. The rancher assembled his ranch hands in order to discuss search strategy. One of them proposed sending out all the workers in dozens of different directions. He claimed that because there were five animals to be located and brought back, scattering in all directions would lead to the greatest number of the animals being found. The rancher instead suggested sending just a few people out in only three or four directions and that they should stop and listen carefully for the animals. He argued that the donkeys would not separate from one another, but would all be found in a group. The workers declared that this strategy made little sense. But the rancher reminded them that a family that brays together strays together.

Jerry was just about the worst employee his company ever had. His job was to operate a document shredder and, remarkably, he was barely competent in handling that duty. In many positions, a marginally capable individual is tolerated if that person is likeable. But not in this instance. In addition to basic performance deficiencies, he was thoroughly irritating due to his continual complaints about his work, his colleagues, his boss, etc. Jerry was eventually fired because he was too outspoken about disliking his work. However, “unsatisfactory performance” was listed as the “official” reason for his dismissal. In reality though, he lost his job because he just wasn’t one to mince words.

Men in physically demanding work (such as construction or football) sometimes take up surprising avocations such as cooking or needlepoint—a change from arduous outdoor exertion to a more sedate indoor activity. Wayne, an actor famous for playing cowboys and various tough-guy roles, maintained a sizable ranch in keeping with his image. But his heart was in an unusual hobby. As long as the weather was clear, he would be engaged in tending to chores on the ranch. But at the first sign of precipitation, he would head indoors and play with his matrices. For reasons unknown, this actor found sources of beauty and harmony in mathematical equations, and he gained great pleasure from multiplying and rotating matrices, and solving simultaneous equations. Some of the older children on neighboring ranches learned of his proclivity and were fascinated by his skill with mathematical games. If he were outside working and children knew that some drizzle was in the forecast, they would come to the fence and sing, "Wayne, Wayne, go array…"

A group of swindlers was operating a boiler room. All manners of stock fraud were being perpetrated with great creativity and effectiveness. They had refined their thievery to a fine art and took great pains to ensure that their customers would not issue complaints to authorities about being sold stock in corporations that were either nonexistent or defunct. To make their scheme work, it was essential to make their clients feel that they had been given top-notch advice. Accordingly, they went out of their way to make their clients feel valued and well looked after. In a nutshell, their motto was to always give the customer a share fake.

The Norse god of thunder decided that his history of being a major god put him in good stead for helping mythological creatures who were just starting their careers or were less known. He actually wanted to train some lesser gods so they would be groomed to take over his job whenever he wanted to sneak down to earth for some recreation. So he asked his father for a temporary leave, and arranged for some Vedic storm gods to substitute for him while he went on this developmental mission.

But this son of Odin proved to be an overbearing, abusive and overly demanding taskmaster. The pixies, nymphs and water sprites couldn't tolerate his dictatorial manner. He offended the mermaids with his crude style. One might expect goblins, demons and ogres to be fairly thick skinned. But they, as well, could not stand up to the snide and sarcastic barbs that were hurled continually in their direction. Eventually, the lesser creatures filed a petition, asking that this god pick up his magic hammer and resume his rightful position in the heavens. They tried to be politically astute, emphasizing how essential it was for this god to return to his normal duties, while never mentioning that he was an obnoxious and cynical Thor mentor.

A clergyman seemed to be suffering from a peculiar variant of Tourette's syndrome. The symptoms only made their appearance when he was officiating at funerals. It was terribly embarrassing when he would blurt out derogatory and disparaging statements which, unfortunately, were often true and very incisive observations about the "dearly departed." The congregants initially considered taking their pastor to a neurologist for sundry tests and evaluations. But instead decided to see whether a newly immigrated sorceress could remedy the problem more expeditiously. After only a brief interview with the minister the enchantress claimed that it would not require elaborate or powerful witchcraft in order to counteract his outbursts. In her broken English, she told him, "We make you weak spell of the dead."

Noting how certain executions and assassinations were intended to "deliver a message," a Mafia torpedo decided to become more elegant and creative in his work. He hired four adolescents and trained them in the art and techniques of murder. Along with those training episodes, he gave them voice lessons and worked with their harmonies until they were functioning as a quartet, singing with crisp and sophisticated arrangements. When requested, a client could hire an execution—which would be handled professionally and with flair. The four killers would visit the home of the victim and, with exquisite tonal structure, sing the message that the client had wished to convey before rubbing out the target.

Naturally it was important for all parties to take steps to secure their anonymity. Their services could not be openly advertised. Nevertheless, the torpedo did have business cards printed. The cards listed a phone number, displayed a graphic of a dumbbell with a "7" imprinted on each of the two weights, and a caption under the graphic, stating "A Weighty Matter." In response to a prospective client's request for an explanation of this cryptic item, the torpedo simply responded, "Fourteen kilograms."

In the days when Russia was still struggling in a communistic stranglehold, laborers in a napkin factory banded together in an effort to secure decent working conditions and improved benefits. Leaders at the manufacturing plant had indeed been taking advantage of the workers, and change was long overdue. But the organization that the laborers constructed proved to be more detrimental than beneficial, almost functioning as an arm of management—to the point of tattling on workers who were especially vocal in expressing their dissatisfaction. In an effort to hang on to what little progress had been made, fellow workers did their best to calm and hush the more strident complainers, and tried to effect more moderated protestations by appealing to the workers' patriotism and national pride: "Silence, comrades. Remember, you're in the serviette union."

A realtor and a building contractor who had enjoyed considerable success over the years decided to have a career change. They formed a partnership and started a men's custom tailoring business. The clientele they targeted were businessmen who, due to body size or proportion, could not be fitted by the typical off-the-rack garments but nonetheless needed quality clothing. Thanks to their professional backgrounds they had no difficulty in deciding upon a company slogan: "We suit to build."

An elderly anchorite was having mysterious physical ailments and was taken to a clinic with the hope that the physicians could diagnose the problem, effect a cure, and send the gentlemen back to his monastery. However, the diagnostic team was unable to come to any agreement on the monk's malady. Some of them were convinced that he was suffering from a virus; others declared that bacteria were to blame. But the majority asserted that the problem was chemical—an imbalance either in hormones or in certain electrolytes that had been caused by the overzealous pilgrim overtaxing himself with too many ventures, resulting in stress, depression, and fatigue.

As a result, the physicians sought the consultation of some biochemists who, although equally bewildered, recommended a "shotgun" treatment strategy. They put the monk on a regimen that featured a variety of medicinal chemicals, with the hope that the problems would be corrected and the monk would be restored to health. When the abbot came to visit, he inquired about the brother's condition and the nature of the treatment in progress. The chemists, attempting to provide a thorough and honest answer, stated, "We should be seeing some improvement soon. After all, we have several ions in the friar."

A chanting technique perfected by Tibetan monks became popular in the Middle East. As with the Tibetans, the chanters were able to produce multiple harmonic frequencies simultaneously. These unusual sounds allowed the chanters to deal with more than one idea simultaneously—to maintain two entirely different matters in consciousness at the same time. There was an additional surprising outcome. It was discovered that the overtones duplicated the compound tones used on telephones in such a way that two parties could be dialed at the same time. Because shop owners in regions of Turkey and Iraq had been having great trouble with some of the nomadic Muslim people failing to pay their bills, this chanting technique became extremely popular: These very busy merchants could practice meditation while at the same time dun pairs of delinquent customers. Thus they could bill two Kurds with the same tone.

There was a textile plant in Bangkok that specialized in putting colored patterns on a huge variety of items, ranging from t-shirts to bedspreads. One day one of the plant workers was found gagged, with his hands bound behind his back, and drowned in one of the vats. The evidence pointed clearly to homicide, rather than to suicide or accident. Given the suspicion that the murder had been instigated by a rival company, the police assembled a roster of employees at all textile plants in town as suspects. At the top of their list were other textile artisans specializing in Thai dying.

Father Christmas had one deviant reindeer who seemed to misinterpret nearly everything that the kindly old elf had ever done. Thinking that he had been abused, mistreated, and forced to work unreasonable hours, this beast managed to agitate all the other reindeer and induce them to share his misconceptions even though, at heart, they knew that all accusations were thoroughly unfounded. They saw no need for any change in working conditions. The deviant reindeer was so successful as a troublemaker that very early one Christmas Eve he instigated a revolt, resulting in all reindeer taking off with the loaded sleigh—minus St. Nicholas. The reindeer were true rebels without a Claus.

An equipment rental agency was having a special event where the cost for renting each tool was being determined by auction. A rather pompous individual was serving as auctioneer. He always delivered a short preamble before introducing each tool and kicking off each round of bidding. So he started, "First and foremost..." and took care of bidding on the rental of a piece of garden equipment. The bidding plodded on through the afternoon: "Our next piece of glorious apparatus...." or "Moving right along to another handy household gadget you couldn't live without..." were the prologues to some quite obscure items. But the auctioneer was so skillful that even specialized and peculiar tools were rented. It appeared as though everything had been rented until a helper discovered one remaining item that had been overlooked in the warehouse. This final device indeed was truly unusual: a shoe form that had been adapted for shaping the seats in lederhosen. Not skipping a beat, the auctioneer held the tool aloft and started his spiel saying, "Butt last not leased...."

A theatrical producer sought to make a major impact on the world of live stage. He hoped to convey a resounding social message through the use of a script that he had discovered. The play was an intergalactic allegory; it called for a special "race" of green people who would perform nude. To achieve the necessary effects, the actors were required to soak themselves in green pigment for several hours. By so immersing themselves, they acquired a pale green hue. Because the color took weeks to wear off, the actors had to be guaranteed two months' wages in advance.

The development of the production had reached the point where there could be no backing off. Several irrevocable commitments had been made, e.g., scenery construction had been commissioned, the theatre reserved, stagehands contracted, and actors thoroughly pigmented. To summarize the fact that all arrangements were in place and were irreversible, the producer sent a terse telegram to the financial backers: "The cast is dyed."

A major supplier of marijuana implemented a scheme with the hope that his profits would soar. Rather than distributing the genuine product to his army of dealers, he purchased bales of donkey mane, dyed it, and then packaged it so it looked like normal packages of dope. The scam worked only until his dealers were inundated with complaints from angry customers, declaring that the latest shipment of loco weed tasted awful and lacked wallop. The dealers subjected the product to closer scrutiny. Uncovering the deception, they united and rapidly reached consensus that the supplier should be seriously threatened with being put out of business. Without warning, they broke in on the supplier, backed him up against the wall and shouted, "Your grass is ass!"

A bullet, still in its casing, was found on the 6th green of a golf course. Although a massive variety of other evidence had been collected, it turned out to be the central clue needed for solving a complex mystery involving international intrigue that culminated in a murder occurring during a Christmas party at the clubhouse. The super-sleuth who unraveled the intricate plot and correctly identified the killer was asked how he came to suspect the clubhouse Santa as the culprit. The detective hummed a familiar tune for a while before breaking into the words, "...and a cartridge on a par 3."

A homeless wanderer who had navigated the entirety of Britain decided to extend his explorations to other segments of the United Kingdom, and managed to mooch a ride to one of the British Isles. His friends, who stayed behind in England, were concerned for the safety of their itinerant friend. He was a foreigner roaming through Dublin and Belfast at a time when emotions were running wild and there often were riots and bombings. Wanting to learn whether their fears had any foundation, they consulted the clergyman at their local parish who, due to the local climate, seemed to endure chronically stuffed sinuses. The pious old vicar replied that their friend would never be truly isolated and at risk. He intoned, with great reverence, that they must remember John Donne's famous words: "Nomad is in Ireland."

A laborer acquired a strong aversion to his job as excavator, and after digging yet another trench with his backhoe, gave notice. He immediately began searching for a new line of work; he had a family to support and was ineligible for unemployment since he had quit his excavator job. He soon discovered that finding other work was virtually impossible. Every other line of gainful employment seemed to require considerable training and specialization. As the days grew into weeks and his savings became depleted, he reached the state of desperation. Eventually he begged for a job as a cobbler's assistant, lying about how much prior experience he brought with him in the craft of shoemaking. It clearly was a last stitch effort.

Following the tradition established by Frankenstein, a team of "mad scientists" collected components from corpses, patched them together, and applied the famous electric jolt to bring the creature to life as a functioning zombie. Their first efforts involved body parts selected for exceptional brawn and great brain power. But these experiments tended to be failures. They had far better success when not striving for exceptional strength or ability. Sometimes various parts failed to operate properly, so they had to devote extra attention to replacing faulty joints, burned out glands, etc.; but eventually they got all pieces fully functional. The end product was a smashing success—to the point that the creature got and successfully held a job on the assembly line at a manufacturing plant, and produced an admirable record of steady productivity.

The monster was polite, well-mannered, and well liked by his coworkers and supervisors. He managed to fit in well, remaining quite inconspicuous until there was an emergency situation. The creature, showing no regard for personal safety (which is logical, given that he could always return to the scientists for repair), rescued one of the middle-level managers from peril. Then, not only did the story of heroism hit the media but also the mad scientists' work became publicized. During the interview in front of microphones and cameras the monster was hailed as a true superhero. Being modest and rather shy, he simply said, "Aw, shucks. Don't make me out to be more than I am. I'm just an ordinary working stiff."

It is a little known fact that in the midst of his writing career, Shakespeare had been challenged to a duel. The dispute was over an utterly trivial matter, but both parties became overly dramatic and a minor disagreement mushroomed into a major dispute. To defend their reputation and pride, each vowed to engage in a duel to the death. Friends of both men intervened and persuaded them to find a strategy whereby they could settle their disagreement without risking a fatality.

Eventually both parties consented that an all-out wrestling match would settle the dispute satisfactorily. To ensure that the conflict would be intense, the combatants convinced their friends to lift all restrictions. Accordingly, there were no rules, with the sole exception that their singlets must remain intact, without rips or tears throughout the match. As Shakespeare's competitor phrased it at the outset of the contest, "Remember. No holes, bard."

A zoology student had the summer job of assisting a naturalist who was collecting basic data on the ravens and shrimps indigenous to one of the Canary Islands. Because considerable tedious work was required, he was one of several students who had been hired to assist a team of biologists in the task of cataloging the various flora and fauna.

One afternoon, all the other students had finished their work early, and had suggested that our friend knock off and join them for a swim and a party at a nearby beach. He was immediately in conflict. He had a large backlog of birds and crustaceans left to measure, and he wanted to impress his boss with his diligence, self-sufficiency, and the quality of his work. At the same time, he felt an enormous need to give himself a break from the redundancy of his work. He found himself vacillating and in a state of indecision. In trying to choose whether or not to knock off work and grab some recreation, he said, "I'll have to weigh the crows and prawns."

An assortment of imps and elves formed a syndicate and pooled their hoarded treasure in order to purchase a major long distance telephone company. The takeover actually was quite amicable. A few golden parachutes were launched, and a reasonable number of pixies and gnomes were installed in corporate leadership positions. The members of the syndicate were delighted at the profitability of their long distance service. The only hang-up, so to speak, was with the customers who continued to find it ironic that whenever they dialed long distance, they were making a troll fee call.

Wilbur had a neighbor who drove him nuts. The neighbor was noisy, nosy, and inconsiderate. The neighbor would borrow things, and, if not forgetting to return them, would lose or damage the items. Wilbur first tried all sorts of subtle and tactful ways to get through to his neighbor. When those approaches failed, he proceeded to try crude, blunt, and gross tactics—but they were equally ineffective. The last straw was when the neighbor messed up his orderly and beautifully maintained tool box. Wilbur was irate. He sought to engage the services of a witch in order to cast a spell on his neighbor—hoping that if the spell failed to change the neighbor's behavior, at least some foul consequences would give Wilbur the meager pleasure of retribution. In seeking his sorceress, he was surprised to be directed to a hardware store. But then, upon being guided to the hand tools area, this source made sense since he was looking for a hex wench.

A woman was preparing for a reunion at her house, the family home, during Christmas vacation. It promised to be a huge event, including her children, grandchildren, siblings, cousins, etc. One problem she faced was working out the logistics of housing all these people. But her main concern was managing food for the large crowd. Most of the meals would be relatively simple self-serve buffet style. But for the Christmas Eve dinner, she wanted to have excellent food and an elegantly set table using her best china, silverware, tablecloths, etc.

In the course of her planning, she ran into a peculiar problem. As part of the meal she planned to serve a tray of cooked vegetables, embellished with a rich sauce. However, she had been told that because the sauce was somewhat acidic, there was a possibility that it could corrode a silver serving platter. Although she was striving for elegance, she did not wish to damage her silver. So she consulted an expert—a chemist who happened to be humming Christmas carols when she went to visit. She explained her wish to have a marvelous and memorable family reunion as well as her concern with the serving dish. The chemist, humming all the while, understood her worry about the platter, sympathized immediately with her nostalgic goals, and without missing a beat shifted to singing, "There's no plate like chrome for the hollandaise."

Most predator cats hunt in conventional fashion. That is, there is a frantic chase that identifies members of the herd that are less fleet. In accordance with selection pressure and survival of the fittest, these are the animals that are caught, killed, and eaten.

However, a band of leopard-like cats, known to be sneaky and devious even when dealing with one another, gained a reputation for using atypical hunting practices that required little physical exertion. Recently they devised sleazy tactics to lure antelopes to their hiding place, where the lazy cats could easily pounce upon the unsuspecting victims for their supper. The senior ranking antelopes called a meeting with the younger and less experienced animals in order to alert them to this new and atypical peril. At the conclusion of the indoctrination, the elder in charge admonished, "And don't forget: Cheetahs don't prey fair."

A posse in the old Wild West had been tracking a band of outlaws across the plains and desert all the way to the coast, where the scoundrels had booked passage on a vessel sailing for Europe. Reaching port just before sailing time, the lawmen quickly boarded the ship in order to continue their chase. Proper legal procedure required the member of the posse placing a criminal under arrest to have a warrant in hand. However, there was only one set of documents available, meaning that even if an outlaw were confronted and caught, he could not be arrested legally. This limitation resulted in a lot of unproductive activity when all members of the posse were in simultaneous pursuit of the miscreants.

The posse was getting tired and frustrated from pointlessly chasing around the ship, so the sheriff in charge called a strategy meeting. He suggested that instead of all posse members running after the crooks at the same time, they take turns, such that only the one lawman holding the papers would chase the thugs until getting tired. He would then hand the documents to another lawman; then another, and so on, until the criminals got tired, gave up, and submitted to arrest. They agreed that it was a fine plan. One member of the posse asked where they should congregate so the runner could relay the materials to the next man. Another deputy piped up that the ship's water closet would be a suitable and convenient location since it was at the only route between the starboard and port sides of the ship. "Okay, men," drawled the sheriff. "We'll pass 'em off at the head."

Young King Cole had long given up the simple pleasures—pipe, bowl, and violin trio—that had amused his predecessor. Instead, he was a technology and media fanatic. He had a bank of television sets mounted on the wall of his great hall plus a set of satellite dishes so he could monitor news reports from all wire-services and from broadcasts of all nations. He certainly was not at a loss for knowledge of current events. But given his great wealth and the extent to which Cole The Second spent surplus funds on self-gratifying devices, a group of prospective visitors were at a loss as to what they could bring as a guest gift. They considered wine, but dismissed this choice, given that the old king had probably built up a massive wine cellar. Likewise, furniture, jewelry, rugs, and animals all would be redundant with what the prior king had accumulated, so these choices were dropped as well. Considering how geographically isolated his kingdom was, one of them suggested that the new king would appreciate seeing some recent magazines and newspapers from outside regions. But then this plan was scuttled by an individual who was aware of the young king's hobby. He scoffed, "That would be like carrying news to Cole's castle."

Gilbert was a famous, recognized celebrity, a member of the English aristocracy. An advertising campaign for an ointment was about to be launched in ancient Palestine, and Gilbert had been hired to serve as spokesman and advocate for its use. But when he saw the script for the ad, he exploded: “I will not make a fool of myself. Rewrite it or I am gone.” The scriptwriters dug in their heels, claiming that it was impossible to modify a single word of their material. Becoming petulant, Gilbert pouted that he would not subject himself to such embarrassment and absurdity, and surely would not “peddle” the ointment, no matter how beneficial it was alleged to be. Turning assertive, he declared, “There is no Gil in balmy ad.”

There was an annual yachting event that had been dominated every year since its inception by the British. The venue of the competition was rotated with the provision that the hosting country was responsible for determining and enforcing all racing regulations. This year, the regatta was scheduled to take place in England. One of the provisions imposed by the hosting yacht club was that there would be no cancellations due to weather. However, a freak storm blew up, dropping golf-ball-size hail shortly before the first race was due to begin.

The Italian team headed a protest, arguing that due to these extreme and severe conditions, the race should be postponed. Privately, the commodore agreed. But being a stickler for proper procedure, the commodore insisted on a formal recorded hearing with a representative of the protesters. "What special circumstances do you claim necessitate relinquishment of this prescription," was the commodore's pompous question. The remainder of the hearing consisted of the two parties singing in alternation, starting with the Italian team's delegate:

"Hail, Britannia."

"Britannia waives the rule."

A banker from Southeastern Turkey was dunning an individual for back payments on a loan. Despite indisputable evidence of delinquency, that person voiced gross prejudice against nomadic Moslems by ridiculing the banker and mimicking him in a derisive fashion. A small crowd gathered, egging on the negligent debtor and supporting his contemptuous behavior. A writer chanced upon this interchange and made an effort to stand up for the banker. This event inspired the author to draft a story in which a courageous lawyer took a strong and unpopular stance against prejudice. The novel, which eventually became a motion picture, was titled "To Mock a Billing Kurd."

The cobblers and bean farmers in a rural community were both prospering. Due to oversupply on the manufacturer's part, the wholesale cost of replacement heels was at an all-time low. As a result, when the shoemakers charged their normal price, they were making an uncharacteristically huge profit. The bean farmers were prospering for the opposite reason. Poor growing conditions that year had resulted in underproduction of all legumes. As a result, the price of beans skyrocketed, enabling the farmers to sell their crops, normally worth next to nothing, for enormous profits. These pricing circumstances led the locals, when wanting to disparage the value of something, to declare that it doesn't amount to a bin of heels.

Some organisms have peculiar life cycles. For example, one huge, aquatic beast is equipped with a tiny ovipositor by which it injects its insect-type fertilized egg into a black bean. As it develops, the larva consumes the inside of the bean; then gnaws its way out, emerging as a dark, unattractive caterpillar. The pupa feeds voraciously on the bean plant, quickly doubling and redoubling its size. It eventually seeks a secure cave adjacent to a large pond or lake where it forms a cocoon and slowly metamorphoses, emerging as an enormous aquatic monster. This novel specimen served as inspiration for movie producers, who used it as a central character in a landmark film: "The Creature from the Black Legume."

Dustin was a genuine polymath. He could speak five languages and could read four in addition. He had accumulated advanced academic degrees in a variety of disciplines, and had engaged in a surprising variety of careers—aviation, medicine, astronomy, paleontology—you name it. Despite his vast erudition, encyclopedic knowledge and his habit of leaping from one field to another, a long-standing interest in electronics and amateur radio did persist. He also had an abiding passion for bizarre wordplay, which he would transmit to acquaintances all over the word via Morse code. Naturally he was known as The Pundit.

A Mexican play director was responsible for a series of summer stock productions that each included material that was explicitly sexual in nature. The director was at the end of his rope, disgusted with the temperamental, conceited, prissy leading men he was forced to deal with. They all were magnificent physical specimens; unquestionably handsome. Even though they all knew their lines and were able to deliver them with excellent timing, each of them was a fussy, overly refined prude, unable to deal with the sexual parts of the script. Each behaved as though he was the best actor on the planet plus the supreme gift to women—while also being absurdly formal, stiff, and precise. The director ranted and raved to no avail. Following another clash with these actors, the director yanked out another fistful of hair and screamed, "I am have it with these prim Adonis."

Landowners in a mythical kingdom came to rely upon some small, fat, furry animals that lived in burrows in the hills surrounding the town. At first the ranchers had been suspicious of these beasts with their furry feet, but soon saw that they were gentle, unadventurous creatures who could be trained to handle manual labor. The landowners found that they could be trusted to perform all the tasks involved with working the acreage—planting, cultivating, harvesting, etc. As a result, the town became extremely prosperous and the landowners became lazy, so thoroughly dependent upon these dedicated workers that they could never bring themselves to work the land again themselves. Observing how the situation had changed with the advent of these little laborers, a New Englander, visiting this region of the kingdom, was heard to remark, "That practice of delegating responsibility proved hobbit farming."

A composer had enjoyed a long and successful career despite the fact that he limited his musical arrangements to reed and string sections only. At first his novel orchestrations were not appreciated and drew criticism. But soon became recognized as highly artful and inventive, his compositions lyrical, flowing, and peaceful. After many years as a composer, this musician decided that it was time for a career change, so he sought work in the movie industry.

For most individuals who had followed the composer's activities and had been touched by the beauty and sensitivity of his works, his choice of film production seemed very strange. As a producer, he was cranking out obscene exploitation films and gory movies that featured shoot-outs embellished with gross and vivid special effects. However, a fellow who had been the composer's concertmaster for 20 years found nothing unusual or surprising in the choice of cinematic material. What else would be expected from someone who had dealt so many years with sax and violins?

In Asia during the middle-ages, an officer of one of the Turkic tribes was routinely brushing his teeth before going to sleep following a busy day of leading an invasion. Suddenly he vanished—disappearing so instantaneously that his toothbrush was left dangling mid-air for a moment before it dropped to the ground. Investigators were baffled and were suspecting foul play until one of them translated the label on the officer's tube of toothpaste: Anti-tartar formula.

Working in his youth first as a bagger, Miles began to move up in the grocery store's organization. Through his work as a stock boy he became fascinated by all forms of food flavorings. This interest led to his serving for years as a buyer specializing exclusively in herbs and spices. Miles was so skilled and successful that he actually became responsible for his own group of stock boys whose duties were devoted exclusively to arranging attractive displays of food flavorings and then guarding the arrangements so they wouldn't get messed up and lose their aesthetic appeal. The store manager was well aware that it was unusual to have so many employees assigned to such a specific and limited set of tasks. But the skill with which the goods were exhibited made such a favorable impression on customers that sales figures were clearly enhanced.

Miles' interests were not restricted to the grocery trade. He had done some amateur boxing and had participated in some tournaments in his younger days. Although his competing days were behind him, he had continuing interest in the sport, and regularly served as a referee. Interestingly, when giving pre-bout instructions to combatants, his work experience would often intrude—as though he were advising his stock boys in the supermarket. So he often would instruct the competitors to "Protect your thyme, et al., shelves."

An old-fashioned teacher from the "old school" became a drug counselor. She was suspected of having once been a nun who taught children in a parochial school, because her favorite therapeutic intervention seemed to be an extension of the time-honored knuckle rapping punishment with a ruler. Rather than aiming for the knuckles, she would whack the clients on the cuticle. Absurd as it sounds, she claimed to have achieved considerable success applying this tactic to individuals being treated for drug dependency. A visiting consultant, quite impressed at how this technique went straight to the heart of the drug addiction problem, declared, "It really hits the head on the nail."

Hockey teams often have international compositions, and the Tavern Saints was no exception. On this team was a huge, evil, burly, newly imported player from Czechoslovakia. As with many individuals who are just learning a new language, this player had started with the dirty words. But unlike many new language learners, he had not expanded his repertoire in the slightest, so the only English that number 88 spoke concerned obscene sexual comments.

The Belfry Devils were slated to play against the Tavern Saints. The game had scarcely started when foul-mouthed, hard-hitting, nasty number 88 knocked the Devil's forward off the play. It was such a violent block that the wind was knocked out of the Devil, who slid into the boards and was knocked unconscious. Getting up and shaking the cobwebs out of his head, he asked what happened. He was told that he had been the victim of a wicked bawdy Czech.

A branch of the United States Department of the Interior was having a barbecue. All the people in attendance were various forms of politicians, clerical workers, bureaucrats, middle managers, political appointees, etc.: essentially, a huge office party. The center of attraction was the barbecue itself, on which only the choicest of cuts from five bison were being grilled. (The bison, of course, had been deemed excess; the herd, of course, had to be thinned, and the timing, of course, happened to coincide conveniently with this party.)

Just as the food was nearly cooked and ready to eat, the assemblage realized that there was a party crasher in their midst. The entire agency had been hounded for years by a grizzled old prospector. He had spent his life searching for ore deposits on government land and periodically sought ownership for some sections, demanding the right to develop a mining operation. One of the bureaucrats, irked at seeing this unwelcome guest (especially when the prospector started crowding toward the grill and pointing to one of the hunks of meat), asked, "What is that old geezer doing?" The answer was obvious: claiming his steak.

After investing massively to buy a house in the suburbs, a family was upset to see that the neighbor on one side had decided to operate a cattle ranch, and was building corrals right next to their property. Then the neighbor on the other side converted his house into a nightclub that played loud and obnoxious rock and roll music into the wee hours. The family's hopes were shattered. Instead of having their dream home in which they could avoid the city and enjoy a serene existence, they had smelly cattle, unnerving music at all hours, plus the added traffic and commotion that both establishments attracted. The family had sunk all their assets into their home. Given the changes that their neighbors had made, they saw a drop in their property value such that they could not easily sell and relocate to a more pleasant and peaceful location. Their options were to stay, and put up with adversity from both sides, or they could sell and take devastating financial beating. You could say that they were stuck between a herd and a rock place.

A sensitive and emotional young man believed, incorrectly, that he had been jilted by his girlfriend. Feeling despondent and being an emotional, dramatic, and rather impulsive individual, he sought a lover's leap in order to end it all. However, the location that he thought to be a major precipice was merely the crest of a rocky hill. His friends tried to talk him out of this futile and hopeless act, declaring that he was jumping to contusions.

Despite sincere efforts to be a good and dutiful wife, a woman nevertheless went through a series of divorces from husbands who each displayed a different major inadequacy. She finally just gave up on married life and decided to put her university training in geology to use, which typically put her by herself in remote locations prospecting for ore.

Eventually she discovered an extraordinarily rich and extensive vein. Its mountaintop location was remote and inconvenient to reach. Furthermore, because the configuration of the ore deposit required difficult and hazardous tunneling at a steep angle through unstable rock, miners she hired rarely stayed on the job for more than a week. Her success in finding an effective foreman to oversee the mine's operation was equally dismal. It all goes to show that a good find is hard to man.

A fan was so dedicated to his favorite soccer team that he brought a skilled goal-keeper from the Ukraine and provided the player food and board in his own home, all at his own expense. After the team won an important tournament, this ardent supporter put on a first-rate reception that was specifically intended to honor the goalkeeper and also the grounds-keeper, who had done an exceptional job of maintaining the turf on their practice field. The event had been planned as a closed affair, limited to just a few people on a guest list. But word leaked out and the party became overrun by hordes of enthusiasts. Rather than spoiling the affair, it turned out that these party crashers enlivened what, otherwise, would have been a dull and stilted event.

Merriment was at a high pitch until a priest walked in. The celebrants immediately commenced to tone down their behavior. The host of the party was concerned that the presence of a clergyman would ruin the festivities, leading people to subdue their exuberance. However, the priest quickly picked up the spirit of the occasion and soon became sozzled. All remaining trepidations dissipated after he proposed a toast in an effort to acknowledge the principal parties and the crashers. His drunken statements seemed to confuse a toast with a benediction. However, it seemed successful and appropriate after he concluded, "...in the name of the sodder, the fun, and the goalie's host."

A linebacker who also was a member of special teams was penalized a record number of times for crashing into the opposing team's punter while failing to block the ball. This football player's limited impulse control appeared in other arenas as well, probably because he was highly competitive no matter what the activity. For example, when playing a friendly game of bridge he became upset when his partner trumped his winning lead—and actually kicked his partner's ankle under the table. One of the opponents saw this and said, "Hey, that's out of line. Of anyone, you should know that there is a penalty for kicking the ruffer."

A cook's entire professional career had been working for a very fussy employer whose taste in food was limited to the most plain and bland food possible. Anything even vaguely in the direction of a casserole was entire foreign. A potato was a plain potato. Gravy on a piece of meat would be unheard of. A vegetable, at the most, would be embellished with a modicum of salt; sauce would be unthinkable.

After a number of years of tolerating such a restricted and boring repertoire, her creative impulses could no longer be suppressed. So one evening, she baked some potatoes with cheese—and was ecstatic over her culinary invention. She could scarcely contain herself when serving supper, and excitedly asked her employer, "What do you think about my creation? What should I call it?" The reply: "Ugh. Rotten!"

Sir William and Sir Charles acquired their honorary ranks in different ways. William, an action oriented person, came to fame through heroism and military service. Charles, a pacifist, had gained notoriety through charitable and philanthropic efforts. Each of them felt that the other's title was unwarranted and had no business having been bestowed by the queen.

As it turns out, both happened to be booked on the same luxury cruise. Considering the limited area, and given that neither man would confine his movements to his cabin, it was inevitable that the two of them would encounter one another occasionally. But when their paths did intersect, they passed by one another in silence, without exhibiting any inkling of recognition—literally, like two knights crossing in the ship.

A temple that served as headquarters for one of the major Eastern religions was far more than a place for chanting and meditation. It also served as a repository and gallery for sculptures and paintings—most of them masterpieces. Nearly all of the followers of the religion lived at the temple, thus providing strong feelings not only of membership but especially family warmth and cohesion.

A visitor to town had learned of the temple's gallery, which was not listed in any tourist literature. He spotted one of the temple members, who happened to be a cockney, and asked for directions so he could view the exhibits. He suggested that the tourist just follow his ears in order to locate the temple. And reflecting his personal attachment, the transplanted Brit simply declared, "'Om' is where the art is."

Over the years a professional toastmaster became progressively more and more upset if he had to observe anything more protracted than a quick, "so long." He simply could not endure watching long, emotional goodbyes. To cope, he usually tried to leave as soon as possible after making his obligatory introductions. His need for quick escape escalated. This intolerance for prolonged farewells nearly cost him his reputation when, instead of providing a lengthy and rousing introduction of a keynote speaker, he simply said, before dashing off the stage, "And now, without further. Adieu."

An association of morticians sponsored a nation-wide embalming contest. Each contestant consisted of a team from a mortuary which would be provided a corpse that had been badly mutilated in a highway collision. Their job, of course, was to prepare the body so it was as attractive and lifelike as possible; so that a surviving family would be proud to have the deceased on display; and so the funeral could allow for an open-coffin service. The competing embalmers—selected to be the most elite and capable in the business—had come from all over the country to this event, and were taking it most seriously. Not only was the winner to receive some exceptional prizes, but notoriety from being declared the best of the top morticians in the country would have monumental professional implications. As one of the contestants phrased it, “We’re really in stiff competition.”

In the fall, a small college would hold campus tours for alumni along with pep rallies for the athletic teams, plus other events to boost school spirit. Over the years, various events had been introduced with the intention that they become permanent parts of the festivities. Few survived more than a couple years. One activity that did remain as a lasting tradition was selection of a woman student to preside over a dance. At the very outset, the contest had been based on appearance and popularity. In recent years, however, the college made a change in the selection process, and based the choice on talent. Each year a different skill was featured.

This year the college decided that candidates should compete by making music using tissue paper placed over a hair comb. As was hoped, the contest generated much interest and the most talented, of course, was crowned at the dance as the comb-humming queen.

A small herring proved to be thoroughly obnoxious due to its persistent whining and over-demanding behavior. Many observers thought that its behavior was simply attributable to parental overindulgence—but that still did not make the creature any more tolerable to be near. It was deeply disliked by virtually all members of their community, to the point that when one of the herring's tantrums resulted in its accidentally landing in a simmering pot of soup on the stove, there was not a single declaration of remorse. Instead, most of the witnesses simply declared, "It served him right, the boiled sprat."

A village was peopled with anchorites in search of religious truths. Becoming a member of this community of troglodytes afforded certain privileges, but involved certain obligations and sacrifices as well. Advantages included use of certain tax loopholes (e.g., declaration of oneself as a religious institution) plus housing conditions that assured complete isolation, which aided meditation. Total compliance with regulations was demanded. Contact with modern mechanical and electrical contrivances was forbidden. Use of only the most rustic and primitive devices was permitted.

Despite these strictures, occasionally one of the hermits would sneak out to the neighboring village and arrange for a chauffeur to take him sightseeing in a large limousine. Both the hermit and driver knew what was jeopardized: the hermits risked eviction and the chauffeur risked heavy fines for contributing to delinquent behavior.

One afternoon the passenger was eager for a wild joy ride over some winding mountain roads. The vehicle skidded and drifted around the curves, eventually attracting the attention of a patrolman. The trooper flagged them down and started to issue a routine citation for speeding. But, then, the trooper noticed the passenger; he took in the bark shirt and disheveled appearance. He was then compelled instead to issue a citation to the chauffeur for recluse driving.

A group of basketball players from two rival teams went on a duck-hunting expedition. One of the players accidentally discharged his gun, resulting in a sizable load of birdshot being lodged in the backside of one of the players from the other team. The victim took it calmly, declaring that it was a familiar and common occurrence. He was often shot in the act of fowling.

A large women's apparel store carried clothing constructed from a wide variety of natural and man-made materials. It was decided to have a sale on all items made of synthetic fiber, which meant that many items needed marking. The boss informed all employees of this plan and assigned department heads various tasks in preparation. Naturally the department heads fobbed off the more onerous and tedious jobs (e.g., making signs and marking the sale merchandise) onto the clerks.

Having just handed a clerk a roll of "50% OFF" stickers, the head of the undergarment department felt slightly guilty due to the enormity of the task. Before dashing off to other responsibilities, the department head tried to raise the clerk's spirits, calling, "Good luck. Don't tag any wooden knickers."

A hipster was ambling and shuffling along the street, humming and jiving; just looking cool. Suddenly a dune buggy screeched to a stop at the corner; it was sporting a massive sound system and was blaring some frenzied bop music. The hipster had never before seen such a vehicle. So, true to form, he performed an exaggerated show of observation—that would make the traditional "double-take" look subtle—and exclaimed, while snapping his fingers in time to the music, "Hey, man. Dig that breezy crate!"

There once was an Earl who ruled a small county. His outstanding virtue was his punctuality. Because of this compulsion to reach meetings before their customary scheduled hour, he had been able to barter most effectively on behalf of his underlings. In time, his county became very prosperous and he was held in highest esteem by his vassals. His lofty status was compromised, however, when this noble leader became infested with intestinal parasites. The serfs and vassals refused to be beholden to a nobleman having a commoner's illness. As a result of continued ridicule and the loss of respect from his subordinates, the gentleman was forced to relinquish his rule to a viscount and to seek a sheltered social position where he could avoid further disgrace and dishonor, thus going to show that the wormy earl always gets the bird.

In a rural farming community all crops had been threatened due to an infestation of larvae. There seemed to be two alternatives. The community could either attack the problem on a temporary basis by applying dangerous insecticide sprays on the fields, or confront the source of the problem. The cause of the problem was an eccentric entomologist who was renting a room to two beetles that reproduced at an astronomical rate, flooding the surrounding fields with their offspring. The farmers were adamant and vowed that a solution to this pestilence was crucial. After considerable heated deliberation in Grange meetings, the townspeople finally reached consensus: They ejected the entomologist, his renters, and his bughouse from their county. Of note was the fact that the people justified their decision by confessing that they simply had chosen the lessor of two weevils.

A program was instituted for members of families of pre-alcoholics. The relatives were trained to speak through a marionette in an effort to induce the imperiled individual to seek treatment. The goal was to transmit a compelling message with such a load of guilt that the pre-alcoholic's destiny would become transformed. Rather than a future of misery, the person would have a healthy, sober, and productive life and be regarded as a valued and welcome member of the family. The program called for family members to be trained in how to operate the marionette and "speak through it" in order to malign and vilify the individual. The intention was to deliver a powerful and compelling message, with the puppet functioning in the role of prophet of inevitable and miserable alcoholic doom.

The relatives performed perfectly during "dry runs," during which the at-risk party was out of the room. However, they were completely unable to function when the pre-alcoholic family member was actually present. The degree of their personal and emotional involvement was just too great, and they simply could not vituperate, even when the puppet was doing the talking. Although several different training techniques were attempted, all failed, with most of the at-risk individuals eventually winding up drunk, broke, and in the gutter. It just goes to show that you can't make ilk asperse out of a souse-seer.

It was asked whether comparatively meek therapists could have any success in treating incorrigible children. To answer the question, a collection of weak-willed psychoanalysts was recruited to work with some intractable youths. As might be expected, virtually no progress was made. The contemptuous patients successfully corrupted and undermined what little authority the analysts originally possessed. Their actions also led to melancholy and gloom in the ineffectual therapists. The stronger the symptoms of depression in the analyst, the greater the likelihood that patients would terminate treatment and discontinue all further contact. These instances of therapeutic failure affirm that brats subvert a shrinking drip.

It is well known that a major goal for adolescents, even those from extremely affluent families, is to seek independence. However, most wealthy youths also express the major fear that steps toward independence would cost them financial support that they wished to retain and which, in their view, prevented rather than facilitated their detachment from parents. Obviously they were wrestling with a serious and worrisome conflict. Fortunately, it was the rare adolescent who elected outright rebellion. Most settled upon a compromise position of semi-independence showing that, in their judgment, half aloof is better than no bread.

A team of management consultants chose to conduct an in-depth and prolonged examination of the organizational structure of a large sample of bawdy houses. Each establishment was scrutinized for at least a full year for such factors as job satisfaction, absenteeism, stoppages and slow-downs for the workers. Also observed were such matters as communication effectiveness and attention to the bottom line for management and leadership. The evidence and observations showed that only a minority of these enterprises functioned smoothly, with positive labor-management relations and high morale. The majority had serious problems which negatively impacted the business: Clients simply did not make the expected return visits. All the problems observed were attributed to an overabundance of administrators. Not only did the number of middle-managers, assistant managers, etc., outnumber the actual work force but also many of these people were unprincipled swindlers. The consultants thus affirmed that too many crooks spoil the brothel.

A local union of laundry persons had declared a work stoppage in order to put pressure on management for changes in pay, work conditions, and a laundry list of other demands. In order to keep their businesses functioning, management recruited and hired non-unionized workers for the same pay and working conditions as the unionized workers had been provided. Perhaps as a by-product of the discomfort of crossing picket lines, these laborers developed considerable group cohesion as well as company loyalty and morale as the prolonged bargaining and negotiations with the union dragged on. Despite some adverse conditions, these "scab" laborers worked 14-18 hour shifts, thus drawing impressive levels of overtime pay. As the emergent leader of these workers expressed it, "You have to iron while the strike is hot."

One Halloween after a long shift at a local gas station, the attendant donned a deer costume and went looking for some action. His first stop was at a nearby raucous party. Failing to hook up with any women and feeling appropriately horny, he soon left and stopped in at a whorehouse. He wisecracked to the madam that he hadn't had much doe. And then more seriously declared that his funds were limited, so he would need to be provided with someone relatively inexpensive. Much discussion and negotiation ensued about cost, quality and duration. Finally out of exasperation, he blurted out a phrase that had been drummed into his head from years as a pump jockey: "Hey, just give me a buck's worth."

The owner and operator of a Japanese restaurant in the downtown business district tried to think of strategies whereby he could increase his noon trade. Even though hordes of executives and staff persons would stream from the office buildings at midday, relatively few visited his restaurant even though the food was good, service fast and courteous, and prices reasonable.

After inspecting the competitors' establishments and reviewing their menus, he formulated a hypothesis: Instead of nutrition, the main purpose for lunch was inebriation. Alcohol appeared to facilitate business negotiations and blunt the hard edge of intra- and inter-office intrigues. But the primary benefit seemed to involve amusement derived from propagation of rumors, idle chatter, and gossip.

The restaurateur's observations led him to develop a new offering patterned after the "three-martini lunch," but geared to a social stratum a few notches lower. He advertised a special lunch for two which, in essence, consisted of a variety of Japanese dishes plus a six-pack of beer which, when split and imbibed, was usually sufficient for moderate suppression of inhibition in verbal self expression. Logically, and in keeping with his competition, he called it his Brew Prate Special.

Shortly after the U.S. military services started widespread recruitment of women, there was concern that ranks of men and women marching together looked irregular. There also was concern that when following a woman, a man might become overly intrigued by what he was seeing—which could cause a distraction during drills. So a slightly deranged old hard-liner who insisted on seeing everything in neat, uniform rows and columns, put out an edict that all women would be required to wear very tight and restraining girdles. In no time, the scream for sexual equality led to a subsequent order requiring all men to wear similar undergarments, but padded in order to create a uniform configuration.

While these changes did lead to a more consistent appearance during parades, they also led to a regiment-wise rumor that was not appreciated in the slightest by those in command. Their displeasure resulted in an immediate cancellation of both orders and frantic efforts to hush the entire matter. These subsequent steps were put into motion the instant the old colonel heard one soldier lisp to another, "We are all members of the United States Formed Arses."

A school teacher, known as a strict disciplinarian, monitored his classroom remarkably well and caught students in their misbehavior when he didn't seem to be watching. Although this teacher had tried to keep his health condition confidential, it leaked out that he was infested with unusual microbes that would migrate to his retina whenever they needed to expel metabolic waste products. Thanks to some chemical synergism, the presence of the discharge enhanced the teacher's peripheral vision. The students, learning the reason behind the teacher's enhanced observational acumen, declared that they always suspected that he had a head in the back of his eyes.

The navy became intrigued by the surface of carp, noting that the structure not only afforded flexibility but special efficiency for moving through the water. The question thus arose whether Mother Nature's design could be borrowed in order to build ships that could move with greater speed and economy. The ship designers noted that sharks had one type of surface, coelacanths another, and gars yet another. In order to examine these structures in more detail, they sent examples of several species to a company that manufactured biology education materials (e.g., teaching aids of oversize replicas of organs such as the eye or inner ear, or perfectly proportional blow-ups of tiny organisms such as insects or microorganisms) with the request that oversize representations of the fishes' surfaces be constructed for study. One could say that the fish that were sent were serving as scale models.

An engraver who worked for the banknote company that prints U.S. currency had a hernia that was giving him enormous amounts of difficulty and inconvenience. He tried a variety of exercises, stretches, diets, etc. Nothing seemed lessen his discomfort. On the advice of his doctor, he tried religion as a stress reduction measure, but got no relief. On a whim, he grabbed the bible he'd been reading and stuffed it into the front of his jockey shorts. To his complete amazement, he experienced his first relief from the nagging discomfort that he'd endured since first getting the hernia. "I should have known all along," he said. "Just like it says on the bills that we print: 'In God we truss.'"

One plastic surgeon worked exclusively with breast enlargement and breast reduction. This doctor believed that most women base their choice of clothing on the body size that they desire, rather than on their actual shape. So one of his idiosyncrasies was to ask patients to bring in a tee shirt; he would then plan his surgery to adjust the patient to the dimensions of the shirt she had selected. He also had a rather novel sliding scale for payment such that the cost was commensurate with the amount of change necessary to achieve the physical proportions that the patient sought. To advertise his services, he adopted an advertising slogan: "We tits you to a fee."

An archaeologist unearthed what seemed to be a puzzling artifact from an ancient culture that was renowned for its polymorphously perverse sexual practices. The item seemed to be a sewing tool having the purpose of finger protection. Because its elongated structure allowed it to emit a crashing sound when struck, it also could have a functioned as a percussion instrument for musical accompaniment. He was entirely familiar with other items and knew their names and purposes. But in this case he was baffled about how to categorize this artifact. The anthropologist was surprised that such an ancient civilization would have created such a multi-purpose device, and sought input from colleagues at other institutions. The answer finally was given to him when describing the item to an old Freudian cultural anthropologist who laughed and said, "Obviously, it is a phallic thimble."

A cop who had spent too many years in traffic detail was the arresting officer in a tremendously upsetting case in which a young woman had been forced to have intercourse with a series of villains. The rapists used a van for commission of their crime. While one of them took a turn driving, others would hold down the victim; then, without the slightest sign of humanity, they would change roles and continue the atrocity while driving aimlessly through the city.

The rapists were pulled over for running a red light by a traffic cop, who issued a ticket. It was not until he heard the moans and cries of the victim that he discovered the brutal crime being committed. The terrible condition of the victim made the cop, unaccustomed to such cruelty, nauseous and put him on the verge of an emotional breakdown.

Once information reached the media, the barbarity of this criminal behavior incensed the general public. Adding to public outcry and anger was the fact that the district attorney was unable to bring the miscreants to justice for committing a sexual assault. The prosecutor nevertheless believed that the officer's citation would hold up in court since the defendants were charged for a moving violation.

An exhibitionist was captured by a band of cannibals who locked him in a cage and set about fattening him up for a special occasion. When festival season arrived, the natives constructed a huge oven in order that they could roast their captive (rather than boil in a soup cauldron, as has been popularized in cartoons). All other preparations had been completed for the great feast. The cannibals paraded their entree around the village. Many of the cannibals came to prod and inspect, and came away anticipating a tender and tasty main course. They then led the victim to the huge roaster. On climbing in to join the vegetables, the victim made a parting gesture of whipping open his raincoat before the lid was slammed down and the roaster shoved into the oven. What the cannibals saw made their mouths water: The exhibitionist had a magnificent, well-toned body. It had been a long time since such a delectable looking dinner had been captured. During the dancing and cooking, nearly all conversation was expressing great expectations about their savory feast.

To the cannibals' surprise and dismay, their main course proved not only to be bland and tasteless, but also tough and gristly. "You can't tell a book by its cover," declared one disgruntled guest. Replied another, "Nonsense. Everyone could see that he was just a flash in the pan."

A starry-eyed young girl from the Midwest came to Hollywood with aspirations of becoming a movie actress. She seemed to be trying all avenues, and was encountering absolutely no success in getting her career under way. She worked as a waitress where directors and producers were likely to see her. Her meager earnings went for acting lessons, taught by an instructor who allegedly had "connections" to the industry. She accepted bit parts in theatre productions. She dressed beautifully and frequented places where movie moguls would "discover" her. Nothing was working.

Then she learned that a man from her acting class, whom she found quite attractive, had been hired for a movie. So, thinking that she could finally launch her career, she competed intensely in order to capture the major part opposite this actor in a movie being made by pornographers. When asked why she chose this sleazy route for launching her career, she replied, "I just wanted to get the role balling."

The mayor and city council gave official permission for Sally Stanford to keep her house of ill repute open in their town as long as it created no public nuisance. There were two primary concerns. First, that the establishment be essentially "invisible," namely that there would be no traffic jams and, in particular, no long lines of customers stretching out from the box office. Second, that there be strict control over transmission of venereal diseases. "This council decrees that Sally may continue to operate her brothel," intoned the mayor, "so long as she minds herpes and queues."

While most bible scholars look upon Moses as a leader and lawgiver who received guidance from supernatural sources, it is a little known fact that he was also the first proctologist in recorded history, specializing in treatment of hemorrhoids. In order to fully understand what happened to this information, it is necessary to remember that descriptions of events can become transformed over time. Especially when stories become transmitted orally, the material seems to drift; some information becomes elaborated, details drop out, etc., and legends evolve. Similarly, when put into writing, mistakes can take place due to reliance on scribes. Hence a minor deviation from an original manuscript can become stable and repeated over generations of copyists. Thus, tales of Moses' medical activities in the bible became distorted due to an erratum. They should have been described as his encounter with the burning tush.

Two rival adolescent gangs, the Blips and the Cruds, decided to have a war, but in a fashion in which no one would risk serious injury. They chose to make use of an old juvenile micturition game, and agreed that whichever gang had a member who could urinate, from a set distance, highest up a wall would be declared the victor.

The combat began following ingestion of enormous quantities of soda pop and illegally acquired beer. Naturally all the dominant members took their turns first. From the outset, the Blips were winning. As the competition continued, no other member from either team was coming close to the mark that had been set early on by the Blips. It looked like a lost cause for the Cruds. It was finally up to Sam, the shortest, weakest, scrawniest kid of them all. The Cruds were shouting, screaming, telling him that their status and honor were up to him. Quaking, he downed additional soda pops until he thought his bladder would explode. He then shuffled up to the line and let loose a stream that thoroughly eclipsed the prior mark. The Cruds were ecstatic. When asked how he managed such a performance, Sam simply replied, “pee-er pressure.”

During a vicious Northerly blow from the Arctic, a group of brass monkeys were conversing with a coven of witches about an acquaintance whom they considered emotionless, unapproachable, and thoroughly devoid of humor—possibly because he was suffering from a collection of tics and spasms. As they all sat shivering around the fire, they agreed, "It's colder than a twitcher's wit."

An Irish gentleman had been imprisoned because he was suspected of knowing the whereabouts of stolen treasure. The authorities were frustrated by his continuing refusal to divulge the location of the riches, and vowed to keep him incarcerated until he produced the information they believed that he had. People for miles around were conjecturing about the location of the treasure. Although many felt sorry that he was being held merely on suspicion, most were relieved that the man remained imprisoned since it was rumored that he had a serious degenerative disease. Because the man was small in stature, people referred to him as the leper con.

Sam's main duty was to handle the intake of new arrivals at a prison by conducting strip searches. One of the incoming detainees was actually an innocent person who was being held for his own protection since he was scheduled to testify against some major organized crime bosses. During the strip search, a fellow prison guard asked Sam whether he, too, would be testifying, i.e., whether he could bare witness.

Karl Marx had consistently expressed disdain for religiosity and organized religion, reserving his most vicious and biting comments for the Catholic Church. He railed about communion; sniped at the way nuns were treated and declared that reverence for priests was absurd, bordering on mysticism. He asserted that the church bilked its poorer congregants out of the money they needed for basic food and shelter. He particularly abhorred the way that the main ritual, performed in an obscure language that no one understood, lulled the more devout parishioners into a blissful trance. In short, Marx declared that mass is the opiate of the religious.

After enduring endless impediments from a string of petty bureaucrats, a developer finally managed to construct an enclosed subdivision having sophisticated security on the outskirts of one of Wisconsin's major cities. Because the homes were reasonably well constructed and their price was not out of line, they sold rapidly with little need for sales pressure—which was surprising because the developer, after his frustrating encounters, had named the subdivision, "Cheesehead Estates." Some tourists driving by the town's suburbs spotted this name and immediately jumped to the correct conclusion that it was a grated community.

It was discovered that the massive upsurge in cosmetic surgery was not just a result of age demographics or some sort of social trend. But rather, epidemiologists identified a rat-borne virus that seemed to be responsible for people flocking to plastic surgeons in droves to get breast implants. This mutated form of rat-borne disease was shown to affect women's hormone system, causing shrinkage of their breasts. Rather than giving this virus a typical label composed of letters and numbers, the scientists simply named it the boobonic plague.

A group of masochists sought to learn how to maximize joy. So following each stroke of a flogging that they received, volunteers reported the degree of pleasure that they felt. A group of observers was responsible for recording the reports plus any additional reactions (e.g., facial expressions, jerks and twitches, screams and laughs) and how soon they occurred following each blow. Demographic, sociometric and physical information was also collected. Among other things, the masochists learned that, in defiance of a stereotype, individuals trending toward obesity were less jolly, pleasant and likeable. The other outcome was that if a blow evoked a groan, then the sooner the individual was struck again, then the greater the reported pleasure. Thus the closer to the moan, the sweeter is the beat.

Andy had worked successfully for years in his firm. He was charged with finding solutions to production problems of the company's clients. Bored with offering the same hackneyed ideas over and over—even though they were effective—Andy began offering more creative and far out answers, which proved to be less successful.

After hearing complaints from too many clients, Andy's boss re-assigned his workload to one of Andy's colleagues who provided proven, well-tested solutions that satisfied the clients. Andy asked his boss to explain why his colleague's work was valued over his own. The boss simply stated, "They're trite, Andrew."

Phyllis Stein had an advanced degree from a prestigious art school, but was currently employed by a company that produced a line of really shabby junk art. She created cutesy salt and pepper shakers, doggies, kitties, figurines, i.e., every type of dust catcher that could be found on display shelves in the most tasteless of homes. Because the products were ceramic, they had to be fired in a kiln that was located near her work station. Hence she had to endure high heat when at her job.

The poor working conditions, lack of satisfaction in her job, plus embarrassment and guilt over feeling that she was preying on boorish fools who bought the company's junk, led Phyllis to lodge a complaint with her boss. He simply replied, "If you can't stand the kitsching, get out of the heat."

The Ottoman Empire relied upon the reports of a network of spies and informants. No wonder they became known as a bunch of stoolies.

A group of pudgy women decided to visit a dude ranch. In order to dress appropriately, they stuffed themselves into plaid shirts and denims. The staff found the sights amusing, and made private comments among themselves. This practice caused no problems until the head of the chuck wagon slipped when announcing the menu for lunch, and described the main course as pork in jeans.

When an aging boxer retired, he decided to open a garage that specialized in modifying cars to clients' tailor-made specifications. He enjoyed chopping and channeling bodies, tweaking engines and transmissions, and inventing fancy paint jobs with pin striping and flames.

The old boxer's hero was one of the most famous managers and trainers in the history of the sport. This idol was the person who had mentored Teddy Atlas and had guided the careers of Floyd Patterson and Mike Tyson. To honor his hero, the former boxer named his shop Custom Auto.

An ambitious aspiring actress was having great difficulty finding employment. Even though she would attend casting calls and all available tryouts, she was never chosen. She became so frustrated that she finally resorted to contracting with an agent who specialized in horror films. He almost immediately got her hired to play one of the vampire's victims in a play set in lower Transylvania. However, she was dissatisfied at being hired for such a bit part.

Rufus the pimp was admired by all his colleagues and competitors. They never ceased to marvel at the great skill with which he managed his stable of hookers. His business acumen resulted in an astronomical cash flow that afforded him the most garish jewelry, outlandish clothing, and fleet of limousines.

Eventually he became bored with endless partying and posturing to keep up his image. One day, shedding the eccentric clothes, he slipped into a seat in a philosophy lecture at a local community college. He loved what he heard. He began attending classes and neglecting his business. His stable of girls got snatched up by competitors, his cash flow vanished, and the loan agency repossessed his vehicles. He eventually had to pawn some of his jewelry and clothes. Nevertheless, Rufus devoted all his time and energy to studying philosophy, earning his degree at a 4-year college, his past career long forgotten. All the other panderers, of course, were convinced that he had his priorities backwards, and accused him of putting Descartes before the whores.

A politician, newly elected to office, made a nuisance of himself with the custodial staff. He was continually pestering them about their work tools and modes of cleaning. He demanded that the janitors use dry mops and push-brooms on floors over more effective methods of cleaning. If anyone complained about his preoccupation with building maintenance, his retort was: Unlike most other elected public servants, I'm keeping my campaign promise to make sweeping changes"

A taxidermist had been requested to preserve, stuff, and arrange a pair of mink so they were in flagrante delicto. The whole idea seemed rather amusing at first. But every time he would get one limb positioned, something else would shift, causing new problems and making the task even more difficult. It was clear that the taxidermist was contending with a mounting problem.

The main form of lunchtime amusement for the guys working at a construction site was to ogle the women who walked by. They would make remarks to one another just loud enough to be overheard regarding each woman's physical assets. The game was snicker and stare. Their foreman absolutely refused to participate in this activity. It was known that he held himself apart and did not participate in this adolescent game. He did not try to make the men stop, but he simply, privately, thought that their behavior was degrading and did not join in even though they all ate lunch together. During one noon break, an attractive woman from the main office showed up in order to deliver blueprints. Not seeing the foreman—and wishing to minimize catcalls and wisecracks—she asked the first worker she encountered, "Please take me to your leerless feeder."

A reptile who had unusual mathematical skill was hired by a casino to work out likelihoods for outcomes at horse and dog races, point spreads for sporting events, and payoff probabilities for other forms of gambling (card games, keno, dice, etc.). He was so skilled that stories started building about his amazing talent and incredible sagacity. It was rumored that he possessed special powers and could do anything. To add to the mystique, the casino constructed a special house for the creature (painted green to match his scaly hide) and paved the path to it in yellow bricks. Hence, he became known as the lizard of odds.

Victor was the manager of a concert hall; he also functioned as impresario, handling details for concerts by the resident symphony orchestra. Surprisingly, he had very limited musical tastes: He only liked music composed in the 1600s. He absolutely adored counterpoint. Bach and Handel were his favorite composers, of course. He almost held the music of Vivaldi and Scarlatti in contempt, scorned compositions from earlier eras, and vehemently denounced music that had been written more recently.

Fortunately, he was not solely responsible for arranging concert programs for the symphony. A committee had done a thoroughly successful job of working with the conductor to choose material that was varied and would appeal to the audience. Programs usually consisted primarily of classical and romantic compositions with an occasional medieval work, a piece or two from the modern era, and perhaps even a "popular" tune.

The concert series continued to thrive, attracting a reliable audience of faithful and satisfied attendees. The symphony was actually showing a profit: Musicians and electric bills were being paid, and the numbers of subscribers to the concert series were showing a steady annual rise. All this did not stop Victor from harping on his personal preferences and seeking change in choice of music, arguing that attendance would increase at an even faster rate if his recommendations were implemented. He begged the committee to stop including the earlier "primitive stuff," limit any music from the classical era, and to prohibit any compositions that could in any way be deemed "modern" or even slightly atonal. Because of the long-standing success of the concert series, the committee simply brushed Victor off, saying, "If it ain't baroque, don't nix it."

An ex-football player gained admission to medical school and, when it came time to specialize, found himself attracted to problems and diseases in the urogenital system. The reason for this interest was not entirely clear, but it possibly arose due to locker-room discussions of sexually transmitted diseases that his teammates had contracted. It did seem a strange specialty for a big, beefy guy with huge hands to choose. Perhaps because of the need for dexterity in his delicate medical work, he tied his own flies for fishing. And because he hated to fish on cold and rainy days, he developed an interest in the weather patterns. He set up his own equipment at home and wound up being a better prognosticator than the weather forecasters on the local media. He was often consulted by friends who wanted to know if their outdoor plans were likely to be spoiled with rain. Because he was such an accurate weather predictor, people referred to him as the meaty urologist.

Carol was a dedicated grave robber. She only excavated the burial sites of women because she was expressly seeking jewelry that the sentimental survivors had left on the corpse. Her main goal was engagement rings, and the highlight of her endeavors was when she came across one with a genuine stone of substantial carat weight.

Unfortunately, she had a rather lonely life. Ordinary people would not associate with her. She found vampires and zombies not to be of her taste (and vice versa). But eventually she discovered that she found great pleasure in the company of satanic beings. She regarded her favorite tune from "Gentlemen Prefer Blondes" as her personal theme song: Demons are a Ghoul's Best Friend.

Every organization has some region where employees can relax for a short break such as a water cooler or coffee lounge. And every such location attracts an entertainer—a water cooler comedian or coffee lounge jester who is oversupplied with wisecracks and wordplay. In comparison to other workers, these compulsive jokers showed increased pathology, exaggerated susceptibility to financial scams, easy victimization by swindlers, curtailed corporate advancement, loss of professional esteem, and reduced economic remuneration. Obviously, a fool and his punning are soon martyred.

The main commercial activity of a remote European town was production of a variety of cheese not found anywhere else in the world. There were a collection of secret rituals that continued to be handed down over the generations. The Chief of the Curds (essentially, the "big cheese") would train his son, who would then assume responsibility for preserving and enacting the superstitious rituals in order to support the town's enterprise. The Chief and his offspring were the only people who knew the special ceremonies and recitations. Those important and revered individuals had the use of a special and distinctive vehicle, affectionately called "Curdmobile," that was easily recognized by all members of the population. For the sake of the town's economic survival, it was essential that no harm come to the occupants of that car. Hence, the rules of the road were that at intersections, every other vehicle would stop, wait, and yield to the Curdmobile. In short, it had the rite of whey.

There was an extreme evangelical religious cult that relied heavily on hellfire and damnation in delivering its message. The sect sought a means for proselytizing and also bringing in new revenue. They hit upon a plan that they expected to appeal to hobbyists and pre-adolescent boys: producing kits containing all the parts and instructions for building electronic gadgets. They put together a wide variety of kits, so people could make devices to measure such factors as radiation, carbon monoxide, wind speed, magnetism, and, of course, a variety of electrical concepts such as amperage, voltage, and resistance. They developed attractive packaging and were careful to provide clear and unambiguous step-wise instructions. At the top of each instruction page appeared a prayer. Next, a list of the necessary tools that should be collected for use, followed by a short admonition, in huge bold-face type, to check once more to be sure that nothing had been overlooked: "Are you prepared to make your meter?"

The only playground near a large city preschool was one that had not been maintained due to budget cuts. It was so rutted and uneven that any ball games would be impossible. Furthermore there was mud where the gravel was missing and potholes with puddles. Adjacent to this playground was a lush, manicured lawn belonging to a private condo association. It was pristine, meticulously maintained—the ideal surface for games of tag and for joyful rolling. But the children were admonished that the lawn was off limits to them, and that they needed to restrict their play to the shabby playfield. This frustration led to strong emotional reactions. Most just cried or yelled, but a few walked defiantly onto the lawn. For their trespassing, they were subjected to severe corporal punishment from stern adults who seemed to live by the maxim, "Spare the sod and roil the child."

Examination of the personal histories of occasional police informants showed their degree of illegal activity to remain quite high. They continue to rob and steal because their earnings as police informants are not regular and are not sufficiently large to provide even a subsistence level of income. Being only occasional and informal informants, they have no leverage and are not able to qualify for immunity from prosecution. These stool pigeons would typically receive three 3-year jail sentences during their lifetimes. In other words, a snitch, in time, serves nine.

In contrast, habitual informers are typically made immune from prosecution. These rather conspicuous blabbermouths provide extensive information on a routine basis in exchange for cash. In essence, these regular informers function as well-paid undercover wage-earners. The downside of this arrangement, however, is that habitual informants have an extremely high likelihood of meeting an early and violent death at the hands of their subjects, showing that the weekly squeal gets deceased.

A director often used horses in his films. He employed two trainers to help achieve the behaviors he needed from the animals. For one film, the director wanted a horse to be trained to look seductive by blinking on cue. The horse would not even blink when trainers blew dust in its face. No matter how many creative tactics were tried and how much effort was expended, the trainers failed to teach this simple behavior.

For another movie project, the director wanted to have a horse that acted drunk and silly. Once again, the trainers faced failure when trying to teach the horse to stumble when signaled. However, the animal did prove sensitive to rotation, so guiding it in a tight circular path seemed to result in prolonged dizziness so the horse would continue to stumble and stagger. The trainers concluded that you can lead a horse to dodder, but cannot make him wink.

A Chinese frog having unusual talents entered college and discovered the field in the liberal arts that absolutely captivated his attention: classical languages. Despite the fact that he was an excellent student performing near the top of his class, upon graduating he soon came to realize that there was little call in the work world for frogs having his training. So despite his proficiency in (heavily accented) Greek and Latin, the only work he could find was in a fast-food emporium. Upon seeing the applicant's sterling credentials, the manager said, "You're hired; hop to it." When his conspecifics would come to place their order, he would always ask, "Flies with that?"

The end of the 18th hole of a famous golf course was quite irregular, making for a particularly tricky green. The land contour sloped at varying angles and the grass was inconsistent in height and texture. Golfers knew that this final hole was a major logistical challenge that required more than a little bit of luck. As a result, the golfers adopted a superstition when reaching that green of bussing their club before addressing the ball. As the players said, "That green is a real kiss putter."

Penelope was not a tightwad or skinflint, but she was definitely frugal, refusing to spend on anything that she considered inessential, irrational, or frivolous. As a result of her prudent nature, she was upset by the strictures of her church, which demanded full burial—embalming and interment. Penelope considered the fees that funeral homes charged utterly deplorable, exorbitant, and inexcusable. She felt a need for religious affiliation, was a seeker after salvation, and believed that the route to salvation called for living a righteous life; but she could not see how it was related to the disposition of mortal remains. Hence, she went in search of an alternative church that still offered the promise of salvation but imposed no contingencies regarding the processing of her corpse. Her search was successful, and she immediately prepaid for the simplest and least costly cremation. As she phrased it, "a penny saved is a penny urned."

The owner of a fast-food restaurant came up with an incentive system having the purpose of reducing turnover and absenteeism of his kitchen staff. Every 40 hours that employees worked earned them points. Once a sufficient number of points had been accrued, they could be exchanged for credit toward airline tickets. Naturally his plan immediately became called the frequent fryer program.

A refugee from a tiny town in Eastern Europe ended up in a large American city where she knew no one and where there were no other immigrants from her town. She was feeling lonely and isolated, especially since her mastery of English was primitive, at best. However, at Thanksgiving time an acquaintance she recognized from her little town moved into a house just down the street from her. The two women were able to support one another, discuss difficulties adapting to a new culture, and were able to enjoy speaking their native language.

At the very end of December there was a neighborhood party and her new friend asked how she was doing. Her response: "Happy near you."

A fellow, diagnosed with inflammatory lung obstruction, was prescribed a bundle of drugs. Despite the treatment, his doctor would still hear wheezing and gurgling sounds in the patient's chest whenever he asked him to take a deep breath and exhale audibly. Further testing revealed that the patient had been misdiagnosed and actually had no chronic pulmonary disease, but rather, a temporary case of bronchitis. He was taken off all the prescriptions and his symptoms disappeared on their own. Clearly, the disturbing and persistent symptoms had been due to the drugs, which caused sigh defects.

A foot fetishist was out of work and becoming more and more down at the heels. His girlfriend and arch supporter told him about a job opening as automobile mechanic on an Indian reservation. So with resume in toe, he ankled down to the service station and hotfooted it to the manager's office. After a little sole searching, it was clear that he was qualified and was hired as supervisor of a crew of Native Americans who specialized in suspension systems. It turned out to be a dream job for him since he was in charge of Sioux and shocks.

A teenage girl was making spending money by illegally extracting mineralized specimens of ancient plant and animal life from a preserve. She advertised and sold the prized specimens through underground channels. She recently had put out the word on six collections, which she coded alphabetically. She had received bids, notified the winners, and was waiting for the purchasers to come by to pick up the materials and to tender payment.

One morning the teenager was upstairs practicing her scales in preparation for her next singing lesson with her mother, an accomplished vocalist. Her younger sister, Amelia, was also home, doing her homework downstairs in the kitchen. Amelia knew of her sister's illegal activities and had agreed to keep them secret.

Looking out, the teenage girl saw a customer approaching the house even though all customers had been told that pick-ups and payments were never to be made during practice time. There would be terrible trouble if her mother discovered her illegal dealings. Her dilemma now was how to keep practicing and at the same time inform her little sister to intercept the customer and to give him the fifth group of minerals.

Then she hit on a scheme whereby she could send a "telegraphic" message. Without pause, and in strong voice, she sang loudly: "Door, Amy; fossil lot 'E'." Then, thinking that she must also alert her sister to consummate the deal by securing payment on delivery of goods, she gave closure to her message by concluding with a resounding, "Dough!"

About the Author

Lou grew up in San Diego, graduated from Stanford University, and then earned an M.A. and Ph.D. from Michigan State University. He taught experimental psychology courses at Western Washington University for 42 years. His research area focused on learning with occasional excursions into other topics, including sport psychology, memory, and humor. He wrote articles for *Worm Runner's Digest* and *Journal of Irreproducible Results* (science humor), and is proud to be listed on editorial boards for *Annals of Improbable Research* and *Journal of Irreproducible Results*.

Lou did his best to become so busy with music that he had to give up his day job—which he happily did. He plays solo background piano music and performs with a variety of ensembles that include jazz standards, world music, and Dixieland.

He lives with his wife Marcia, who is extremely tolerant and supportive of his music and writing activities. They have two adult children and one granddaughter.